A41

1466 F
Wh

Walls of Jericho

MARGARET WHEELER

With a foreword by

DR KATHLEEN KENYON, c.b.e.
DIRECTOR OF THE JERICHO EXCAVATIONS

and sketches by
THE AUTHOR

READERS UNION
AND CHATTO & WINDUS
London 1958

TO MY MOTHER
MARY COLLINGRIDGE

This RU edition was produced in 1958 for sale
to its members only by Readers Union Ltd at
38 William IV Street, Charing Cross, London,
WC2, and at Letchworth Garden City, Hert-
fordshire. Full details of membership may be
obtained from our London address. The book is
set in 11 point Walbaum 1 point leaded, and has
been printed by the Alden Press (Oxford) Ltd,
Binsey Lane, Oxford, and bound by Messrs
Webb & Co Ltd, London. It was first pub-
lished in 1956 by Chatto & Windus Ltd

Foreword

PERSONALLY, I have found this book wholly delightful. It may be that I am prejudiced, that the incidents described seem particularly real to me, since I took part in so many of them, or at least had them recounted to me very much at first hand. But I can't help feeling that Lady Wheeler's vivid descriptions and delightful drawings will make them seem real to many others. Moreover, the very way she has told the story is a reflection of the way of things on a dig. She flits easily from the historical framework which our excavations are gradually building up and filling in, to incidents such as a wedding in the Refugee Village, the ordeal of the electrocuted photographer, and a midnight feast on the shores of the Dead Sea. That is dig life. During most of the time, we concentrate on distilling history from the reluctant elements left by the crumbling ruins of the town and cemetery. But a potent solvent in the brew is the morale of the party. This is enormously sustained by the interest of our surroundings and the lighter moments of our annual three months at Jericho.

This book, therefore, may help to give a picture of what goes on on a dig. The world at large seems to be divided between those who think of archaeology as conducted by desiccated elderly professors, poring through microscopes at potsherds and flints, and those who regard it as a wild adventure searching for buried treasure, carried out by picturesquely attired young men. Both views are far from the truth, and the present tale may do something to give a true picture.

Amidst the anecdotes and lighter touches, the fact that the author has gone to considerable trouble to ensure that the archaeological framework is accurate may not always be apparent. But it is nevertheless so, and readers may accept this book as an interim outline of the finds that the mound of Jericho has revealed. Other accounts, weightier and certainly duller, will appear, but meanwhile *Walls of Jericho* may serve as an introduction to the exciting discoveries we have made at the site, and as a description of the sort of life we lead while making them.

KATHLEEN M. KENYON

Jericho
1956

Contents

Plates

Acknowledgments

My thanks are due to many who have assisted directly or indirectly in the preparation of this book. Foremost among them is Dr Kathleen Kenyon, Director of the British School of Archaeology in Jerusalem, and of the Jericho Excavations, whose guidance and encouragement have made it possible. To Professor F. E. Zeuner I have taken many 'geochronological' and other problems, and his patient help has been unremitting. Miss Olga Tufnell and Miss M. V. Seton-Williams have liberally shared with me their specialized knowledge of the Near East, and Miss Dorothy Marshall, Mr J. Carswell, Mr P. Dorrell and Mr R. Rawlins have generously contributed illustrations. Most of the photographs are reproduced by kind permission of the Committee of the Jericho Excavation Fund.

I have also to thank Dr W. F. Albright for permission to reproduce from *The Archaeology of Palestine* (a Pelican Book) the figure on page 119.

CHAPTER ONE

The Spring

THE roads from Beirut are fairly good, and the cars are those monstrous gleaming limousines that combine luxury and vulgarity so perfectly.

I reclined on my jade green leather upholstery, packed firmly in beside two delightful but portly Arabs. In front with the driver two more were seated. I was of the party and yet, unfortunately, remote from it because neither they nor I shared a language.

We wound up and over the beautiful Lebanon mountains, driving eastward into the morning sun. There was snow on the heights, and at one point we passed a busy little téléférique taking keen skiers to the slopes above us. But the chill and gleam of the high mountains did not last for long. We swung downwards into the plain, only to climb again and traverse the Anti-Lebanon still farther to the East.

By this time I was getting on very well with my travelling companions. We had established a *rapport* through cigarettes. Every half hour somebody rummaged in a pocket and produced a packet, and I was included in the round. I think we all felt that cordial relations existed, but the difficulty here was the fact that I do not think they liked my English variety and I certainly could not abide their Harpsichord, or whatever the name was. So when rummaging-time approached we developed the technique, in self defence, of all rummaging simultaneously, and with a smile we would each take our own. At least we were smoking together.

I tried at one period waving my arm towards a village and saying 'Lovely'. They looked puzzled for a little and

11

then smiled. I did not think it had been a success and I did not try again.

We had not much difficulty with the Frontier Post, and in no time we were in Syria, following the green tumbling Barada into Damascus. There was half an hour for lunch and then we all reassembled for the long and rather dreary journey southwards. This is a four-hour drive along the flat and uninteresting plateau. The Frontier Post into Jordan created a diversion – and, alas for all of us, our driver tried to enliven our time with music. Persistent and grotesque were the noises that came from his wireless. Tired, battered, weary, we were deposited in Amman, the capital of the Hashemite Kingdom of Jordan.

My travelling companions melted away; how I envied them their easy conversation with their fellow country-men as I negotiated painfully for a local taxi to take me on to Jericho. One buys a seat in a taxi – wonderful, I had achieved that, and I was seated, waiting hopefully to go. Time gently slipped along. No one took the slight-est notice of me except two or three small boys who wanted to sell me bread-rings, sticky sweets and awful little celluloid toys. I isolated myself completely from this busy world by shutting all the windows. Eventually our taxi driver returned; he had been scouring the streets for one or two more passengers. Everyone bundled aboard and we rattled off. Our driver still hoped to catch more prey: he leaned well out of his window and bellowed 'Ariha, Ariha' as we wound our way out on to the Jericho road. Ariha is the Arab name for Jericho.

We were on the last lap, westward now into the setting sun, dropping from the heights of the Transjordanian Plateau down, down into the great Rift valley twelve hundred feet below the sea. At one point on the road there is a large white notice that boldly proclaims 'Sea Level' or, in Arabic 'The Roof of the Sea'. But still we continued downwards to cross the River Jordan about eight miles upstream from the Dead Sea.

The Jordan – have you a private vision of that river in your mind? I am sure it bears no resemblance to reality.

The real Jordan is a muddy meandering stream of no manifest distinction amidst frustrating swamps of tamarisk and willow. The river and swamps are hemmed in on either side with mud deposits, where everything is dead and still, and nothing grows. These 'bad lands' possess an eerie quality. It is almost with relief that one emerges from the labyrinth of mud on to the straightforward desert slope of the valley.

Jericho lies at the foot of the western escarpment, a rare oasis in this wilderness. Here the unfailing Spring, which will be the focus of our story, has acted like a magnet to plants and man. Over seven thousand years ago it tempted him to build the earliest town as yet known in the world. Seven years ago it became the centre of a packed mass of bewildered humanity for whom no other refuge could be found. Nearly one hundred thousand refugees from across the Israel border are based on Jericho.

We drove in the gathering dusk through the busy little modern town to the very source of the Spring. Towering up above the pool is the mound of the ancient town – and there at last was the Camp House, the headquarters of our expedition.

Dogs, cooks and watchmen came bounding out to meet the car. In no time I was stepping across the two or three shallow streams that flow from the Spring and on to the small island on which the house is built. It was originally a mill-house constructed about 1850, and it has great character. There is an outside staircase that leads to the mess-room and drawing-office. Below there is a kitchen, and an annexe which we use for the Director's office, pottery rooms, storage, photographic and conservation rooms. We have never ceased to bless the good name of Awni Dajani, the government Inspector of Monuments who installed us here.

I made my way up the stairs and into the mess-room, and there they all were – my future fellow-workers. It was excellent to be back. Dinner was just over and it was that period of calm chatter before a resurgence of movement takes everyone off about his business.

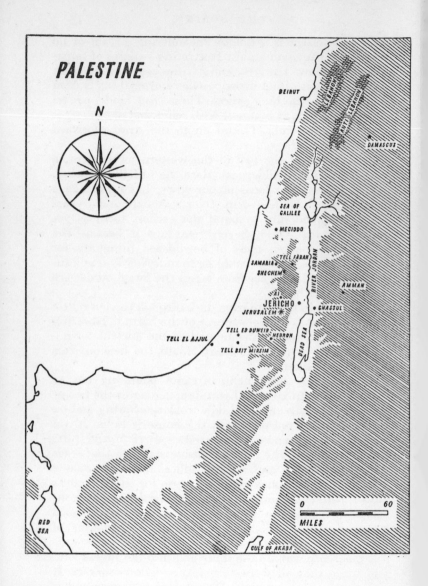

PALESTINE

N

BEIRUT

DAMASCUS

SEA OF
GALILEE

MEGIDDO

TELL FARAH

SAMARIA
SHECHEM

AMMAN

AI
JERICHO

JERUSALEM

GHASSUL

TELL ED DUWEIR

TELL EL AJJUL

HEBRON

TELL BEIT MIRSIM

DEAD SEA

RIVER JORDAN

LEBANON

ANTI LEBANON

0   60

MILES

RED
SEA

GULF OF AKABA

On entering this mess-room two things strike the eye: beards and bottles.

What is it about expeditions that produces this urge to grow a beard? Or do all men secretly long for the opportunity to burst forth, but only on expeditions find people long-suffering enough to put up with the initial stages? Anyway, there were the beards: magnificent red ones, and some mere wisps of things.

And the array of bottles! Each person has his own supply: there is no social duty to offer drinks round because experience has taught us the impossibility of sharing with everyone in the mess-room in the evening. There are, of course, delightful exchanges, but it is quite in order to come in after ablutions before dinner, pour a drink, and sit and savour it with four or five thirsty letter-writers in front of you. The contents of the bottles have an unconventional quality too: they are usually the local brew. A formidable liquid, called *arak* but bearing little resemblance to the usual drink of that name, is favoured mostly. It can be used as a disinfectant for Jericho sores as well as for an apéritif. There is a brandy, too, which you keep specially for the people who have irritated you that day; and the fruit juices, that go with gin, drip like treacle from the bottle and remain in little gobbets at the bottom of the glass until you stir them well with water.

I had gin, lemon gobbets and water that first evening, and an excellent dinner was brought from our primitive kitchen and placed in front of me.

It was delightful to see the old friends and to meet the new. There was Charles, a 'site-supervisor', tall and lanky. He deplored the fashion for beards and could be seen behind the reeds any morning energetically scraping off the unwanted growth. His weakness lay more in a sartorial direction. He sported Turkish, black and white, home-spun shirts which no doubt would have looked very fetching if he had been a good bit smaller or the shirts much larger.

Next to him sat David, who was really just a pair of blue eyes in a ginger thicket. Occasionally the south end of the thicket moves up and down and we know he must be talking, but as his voice is soft, we do not always hear him in the uproar. Occasionally the north end of the thicket is covered with a green knitted tea cosy and pompon, and we wonder if it is possible that his head, buried beneath, can be feeling cold.

There was Nancy, the photographer: an Australian like myself, small and determined; Cecil, in charge of conservation, excellent in an argument; and Dorothy, in charge of the pottery room and records. Dorothy is from

Bute and we Sassenachs have often trembled when, in some thoughtless moment, we have hinted that Scotland is, maybe, a touch peripheral.

Beyond all these sat Oliver, the surveyor, with a moustache that an Italian organ grinder would have been proud to call his own. It was rivalled only by Todd's.

Todd was a Fulbright scholar from South Dakota and affected a 'Walrus'. I marvelled that anything so perfect in the way of a 'Walrus' could have been cultivated in the mid-twentieth century. He was in charge of one of

the trenches on the dig, and he brought to our small world a repertoire of American folk-songs that delighted everyone. Many a time our 'musical' evenings have been saved from mere hullabaloo by Todd, who would sing us songs from the Middle West and the Mississippi.

And there was John, the artist, in his grandfather's trousers. He was very proud of these white spindly 1890s, with their tapering legs and white embroidered buttons.

Opposite sat Diana, in charge of the excavation of the tombs; and Peter and Alex, site supervisors, and Vivienne

the housekeeper, with Mohammed on her left. Mohammed is a young Jordanian from the State Department of Antiquities. His zest for gaiety is infectious. He will sing us Arab songs far into the night.

At the head of the table was Kathleen Kenyon, the Director of the Jericho Excavations. She rules us all, but the stray pariah puppies who seek sanctuary in the camp rule her.

In Arabic the title Madam is Sitt. So Kathleen Kenyon on the dig is known as the Great Sitt. We all are minor Sitts – Sitt Diana, Sitt Dorothy and so on. The men are merely Mr Todd, Mr John.

'And what is the news of the dig?' 'Are there any good tombs?' 'Tell me everything.' So it went on. Eventually we took our hurricane lamps and scattered to our tents.

Dawn. I awakened early, unaccustomed to the sound of

water which was cascading past the door of my tent. The Spring of which I have spoken was a stone's throw away and the water leaves it in two channels on either side of our Camp House. Across the valley the sun was rising over the mountains of Moab and to the south the Dead Sea gleamed like a sheet of silver at that hour. We seemed to be closed in here in the Jordan Valley by wild and treeless mountains, made lovely by the dawn. Beneath them lay a valley no less barren, but eloquent of the strange geological processes that have gone to the making of it.

I do not know if geology has the same effect upon you as it has upon me, but the very words Oligocene or Carboniferous turn me into marble; I know that a far-away look comes into my eye, and I hear myself say 'Oh really!' I think one's mind is stretched too far in trying to comprehend millions of years and mountain ranges popping up and weathering away. And then all of a sudden before you know where you are, everything is submerged, and you begin all over again.

There was a charming little film in the Festival of Britain. It was down in a basement and I suddenly came across it flickering away for two small boys. I joined them. The film showed England being made. Mountain ranges came up and down like caterpillars on the march; seas invaded and retreated and then there was an appalling hiccough, and the land mass submerged. The two small boys and I were looking at the map of England. A calm impersonal voice told us that millions and millions of years had been telescoped into ten minutes. It was a very good little film.

I wish I could begin with such a film of the Rift Valley in Palestine. But I will try to simplify it all in words and make the millions of years slip past with the same rapidity.

Jericho, as yet the earliest town known in the world, lies in this Rift Valley, and the fact that it is situated on the line of the rift is most important. We should not have known many of the details of the lives of the Jerichoans if it had not been for this fact.

First of all you must visualize in this area a wonderful thing called the Original Mass, existing in pre-Cambrian times, well over five hundred million years ago. One must begin somewhere, and a thing called an Original Mass is a very satisfactory thing to begin with. It was made up of crystalline schists and grey granite, and as the millions of years rolled on it was flooded and flooded. Eventually it was topped with sandstone.

When next we need to take it seriously we have come to a period called the Lower Cretaceous, a mere one hundred and thirty-ish million years ago. Then the whole affair was submerged, and, while it lay happily out of sight under water, limestone was formed by billions and billions of organic remains floating gently down through the water and settling below. This operation continued until the Lower Eocene (fifty million years ago). During this period the sea receded a little and there was some erosion in the west of Palestine. Rather monotonously the sea then returned; we know what is going to happen now — more limestone. Eventually in the north the land began to emerge, but in the submerged south pressures were being exerted on the sedimentary deposits which were now a thick crust on the Original Mass. They began to fold.

This brings us almost to geological yesterday, the late Oligocene or Early Miocene, about thirty million years ago. At this stage a dramatic struggle occurred. Tremendous pressure was being applied to the sedimentary crust, which arched and writhed into curving folds running north-north-east; and on the west there was a southward movement of the crust, while the Transjordanian block remained firmer.

All this was more than any buckled sedimentary rock could bear and there were tremendous fracturings and strong vertical movement resulting in the Jordan trough. At first this was divided into two basins — in the north a freshwater lake and in the south a bitter lake. But still the pressure continued until one can almost hear the Jordan Valley saying 'All right, I'll drop out of the struggle'.

In the Upper Pliocene (about two million years ago) the floor of the Dead Sea dropped about five thousand feet below the Eastern escarpment and two thousand six hundred feet below the level of the Mediterranean.

It must have been such a relief when the great struggle was over and the Valley gave in. The Rift runs for two hundred and fifty miles from the Palestine-Lebanon frontier to the head of the Gulf of Akaba. And it varies in width from two to fifteen miles. Minor adjustments and earth tremors have been occurring all the time. In 1758 the great pagan temple of Baalbeck was wrecked and at the same time the floor of the cave at Bethlehem was cracked. In 1929 many buildings in Jerusalem were destroyed. I am told that on a seismograph this area always shows a quiver. But save for minor adjustments we may now leave the defeated Valley in peace until such time as man built his first town beside the Spring.

Beside this Spring stands the great mound of ancient Jericho, hereafter called the Tell. Tell is the Arabic word for a man-made mound of any period. Such mounds vary in size and texture, but mud plays an enormous part in most of them. They are the accumulation of a long succession of towns or villages, each raised upon the débris of its predecessors. These mounds owe much of their height to the fact that the buildings were commonly constructed of unbaked bricks, easy to make and sufficiently durable in the dry Asian climate, but liable to dissolve into thick layers of dust.

Always mud bricks were being brought into the area for patching here, rebuilding there. A house would collapse, it was levelled, and another built on the remains. Rubbish-pits were dug, filled and sealed. And during all this process the household goods of the people were being broken, lost, buried and forgotten.

At Jericho the enormous grey mud mound is now four hundred yards by two hundred yards and stands seventy feet high. It is a history-book of the last seven or eight thousand years. But one has to read the story in reverse, because the remains of the earliest dwellers near the Spring lie buried at the bottom. So as one digs down from the top one begins with the later folk and reads the story backwards into the remote past.

In all, six areas are being dug into the mound during the present excavations: three of these are great trenches. They are fifteen or twenty feet wide and over two hundred feet long, and when our work is finished it will be possible to walk on the surface of the natural rock from outside the Tell, where man has never built, into the centre of the mound. Towering up on either side will be the accumulation of the centuries, and it will be possible to see the procession of towns and defences piling up one upon the other. It is a wonderful thing to see, a great cutting like our Main Trench at Jericho. This trench has already at one point gone right down through the débris of the years and reached the natural rock, upon which the first town dwellers built themselves a defensive wall and inside the wall a town.

Who were these people? The question is an important one, for they were the first, as yet known, to build a defended town. Before our Jerichoans, there must surely have been humbler efforts at defence and communal living? But, if so, these earlier efforts have yet to be found. In present knowledge, if not in fact, our people arrived at the Spring with revolutionary ideas. In the waters they had found security and inspiration. With this aid they would now cultivate and abide. For hundreds and thousands of years man had lived by food-gathering; he had been dictated to by nature. Now he was beginning to command. Now, he would sow and reap and store his harvest in his new citadel. His wanderings were at an end.

Before this, about 8000 to 6000 B.C., earlier peoples, whom we call the Natufians, may have practised a primitive agriculture. But they were essentially food-gatherers and lived mainly by hunting and fishing. Their remains have been discovered in caves on Mount Carmel and at an open site en route from Palestine to Egypt. As well as the many flint arrow-points and bone fish-hooks found at their sites, there are also flint sickles and other flint tools which are thought to have been picks or hoes for breaking up the ground prior to sowing. Theirs was not a settled agricultural life. They may have sown in the spring and then continued their hunting activities, to return in the autumn to reap.

The Natufians were the vanguard of the revolution that was brought about by our Jerichoans.

Farther to the East, beyond the Tigris at Qal'at Jarmo, there is a village with some similarity to early Jericho, and Jarmo shares the honours with Jericho of being one of man's earliest villages, but it is very much the poor relation. Jarmo has no defensive walls.

So there we have the picture – at long last man manages to lead a relatively settled life. He has left the Palaeolithic – the old Stone Age, together with its Mesolithic or Middle Stone Age successor behind him, and has entered into the period known as the Neolithic or New Stone Age. The accepted definition of a Neolithic people is a *food-producing* people using stone implements and without knowledge of metal.

The Neolithic period occurs at different times all over the world. In England in 6000 B.C. we were still very much in the Mesolithic and had to wait well over three thousand years before we became food-producers and began to lead settled lives.

CHAPTER TWO

The First Inhabitants

(6000?–4500 B.C.)

AT the Camp House we all get up at six-thirty and
gather in the mess-room for a sepulchral cup of tea
and bread and butter – or rather bread covered
with a yellow grease nick-named Substance. (One of our
kind supporters, having been a guest at the site for three
days, is increasing his donation by £10 so that we can say
farewell to Substance and buy Australian tinned butter
instead.)

At seven the day's work begins. The site supervisors
make their way up on to the Tell to take charge of their
individual trenches. It is a pleasant sight to see them
plodding up on to the mound, each surrounded with his
own group of lighthearted, irresponsible, noisy ragamuffins – his workmen. In fact, a good half of the duties
of a site supervisor is to see that his pickmen, shovelmen
and basket boys keep moving. It is a task that never
ceases, and each supervisor develops his own technique.
David always spoke in a quiet voice, as if inviting the
men to continue work. And the miracle was they accepted
the invitation. Charles was far more noisy, and, although
enjoyed by his gang, often threatened to 'Flog the Lot'.

Pretty little Alex ruled her group with magnificent
authority. The prize juvenile delinquents of Jericho
became fairly docile basket boys when she really gave
them her full attention. But they were artists when the
demon entered into them to go slow.

The idea is perfectly simple. The supervisor indicates
the areas to be dug and the pickman digs through a
certain amount, breaking up the earth, keeping an eye
open for 'finds'. He then stands back while the shovelman
fills up the baskets which are taken off in orderly succession

by the boys, and the earth is thrown on the dumps well away from the cutting. When any depth is attained, the boys are stationed on the stairs and the baskets handed from one to the other until eventually they can be emptied at the top. The basket is then thrown down to the shovelman to be filled again.

Once one has encouraged a group to work, or 'flogged the lot', this ideal pattern works rhythmically for a little while, but somehow, imperceptibly, hitches occur. All the baskets pile up on the dump with most of the young scallywags smoking and gossiping up there with them. A roar from the supervisor below brings a shower of baskets down into the trench again.

And there are of course contretemps: these are a favourite pastime. A contretemps can be indulged in at any moment and there is a sliding scale of vigour suitable for all occasions. Boredom can be banished in a moment with a really good fight half way up the staircase. Tormenting the supervisor is half the game.

The day after I arrived, the Great Sitt took me for a round of the Tell so that I could be given the picture of what was going on. As she spoke she used archaeological technicalities with an easy familiarity which, before going any further, I will explain. They represent the rather arid terms into which the story of the Tell must be divided if its sequence in time is to be understood. They are as follows:

6000 (?) B.C.   *Pre-pottery Neolithic*
                     Food-producing cultures using stone
                        implements but with no knowledge
                        of metals or of pottery.
4500 B.C.   *Pottery Neolithic*
                     Cultures using stone implements, with
                        no knowledge of metals but familiar
                        with the manufacture of pottery.
4000 B.C.   *Chalcolithic*
                     Cultures using mostly stone imple-
                        ments but with some knowledge of
                        copper and a developing ceramic.

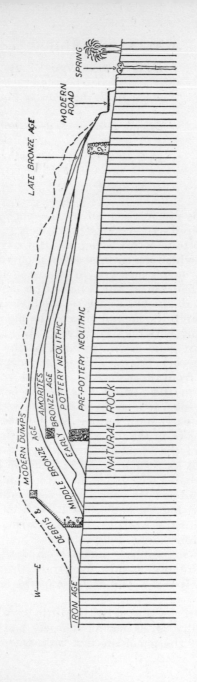

3000 B.C.	*Early Bronze Age*	Pottery and metals.
2100 B.C.	*Amoritic Tribal Period*	Pottery and metals.
1900 B.C.	*Middle Bronze Age*	Pottery and metals.
1580 B.C.	*Late Bronze Age*	Pottery and metals.
1200 B.C.	*Iron Age*	

These periods are represented by the purely schematic and unmeasured section on the previous page.

At the bottom of my schematic town you see the natural rock which was covered seven thousand years and more ago by man's first known efforts at a town wall. With the exception of the Chalcolithic and the Late Bronze Age, all the phases are represented in our Great Cutting through the mound, and at the moment we are concerned only with the Main Trench because it is here that we have gone down through all the layers and come to the rock below. This is at a depth of about seventy feet from the surface.

Standing on the natural rock at the bottom of the cutting is a solid well-constructed stone wall, a monument to the early town builder. As I gazed down at it that morning from the top of the mound, with my feet in the dust of the Middle Bronze Age, I could not help but marvel at its regularity, and ponder on that remote Neolithic Urban Council that had commanded its erection. The boulders are very large, some of them up to three feet in length, and must have been difficult to transport from the wadis in the escarpment half a mile away. The stones are merely unshaped lumps, but have been placed in regular courses with a slight inward slope, and the wall stands, even now, to a height of twenty feet. It was a *tour de force* of the Neolithic site supervisors.

As the centuries slipped by, the little town grew up on the mud stilts of its earlier houses, and the débris cascaded over the top of the first wall. One can imagine the city fathers holding anxious conferences. What was to be done? Houses were going up everywhere inside the town, and it was obvious they could not be contained inside the old ancestral wall. They decided they must build the old wall higher. So up and up the town crept, and higher and higher the mound with its crowning walls. Later a tower was added, but since there was no suitable platform outside the defences, they commanded it to be built on the inside – and so we see it now, a solid oval turret glued to the back of the town wall. It was great good fortune for us that the line chosen for our Main Trench should strike the tower; so easily could we have missed it. We do not know, of course, whether this tower is a unique feature of these early defences or whether there are others buried deeply in the Tell along the line of the city wall.

In time the housing problem became more and more acute. It was a prosperous little town of nearly eight acres, and within the walls there may have been about three thousand people. We can estimate this number because we have traced the limits of the town and know how closely packed were the houses; and, judging from an Arab village of today, houses packed thus and thus over an area of eight acres would shelter about three thousand souls.

Those ancient Jerichoans felt the need to expand. It must have been a great undertaking to extend the town, but nevertheless we see that this was the decision taken at the time. The western wall was buried as they levelled up the débris on the slope outside the old city wall. New buildings spread out and down the slope; a suburb had been created, and possibly a new defensive wall enclosed the area. But of this wall we have no trace. If ever it was there, later people dug it away when they sheared off the slope of the Tell for their own defences. We see these early Neolithic buildings stretching out over the old wall and down the slope, and then they abruptly cease. Middle Bronze Age engineers, thousands of years later, sliced away the limits of that prosperous expansion.

The buildings in the suburb are of the same type as

were built both before and later; above them the Jerichoans built a large rectangular room with curved annexes at either end, which we have called a Temple. It was eighteen feet broad – as yet we do not know the length – and it is the grandest Neolithic room ever to have been found. Most of the floors in the town at this time had been plastered and then burnished to a smooth and silky finish, and the Temple floor was no exception. In the middle of it we found a small rectangular basin, also lined with plaster; it had been stained black by smoke and burning.

Here, I must warn you, archaeologists have a weakness. They love ritual. Things called 'cult objects', 'mother goddesses', 'sacrificial this's and that's' keep cropping up all the time. The wicked might even suggest that this is a very good way of giving names to things about which one has not a clue, and the wicked would not be too far wrong. But, on the analogy of modern primitive tribes, nearly all such unrecognizable treasured possessions are, in fact, charms, amulets, evaders of the evil eye and so on. So I will not go as far as to say it *was* a sacrificial or ritual basin; but it stood a fairly good chance of being one. What did they burn in the basin? Alas, there were no remains; we shall never know.

In time the Temple was abandoned and fell into decay. Perhaps our townsmen were not bothering with their communal buildings, or perhaps the area of the suburb was too much for them and was abandoned. They still built higher up on the mound; and then disaster overtook them. Many of the citizens died and were buried in shallow holes in the collapsed débris of their homes. It may have been massacre. Had they, in fact, never built a wall round the suburb? Was the western side of the town open to attack? On the other hand the bones appear to show no signs of violence. Was it rather plague that struck down the inhabitants? In the shallow graves among the ruined houses there were the bodies of men, women and children.

As I looked down on to these levels that first morning, when I was being taken round by the Great Sitt, my eyes flitted from one sad little group to the next. Some were buried alone in a crouched position with arms flexed on their chests, some were in groups of twos and threes, and some appeared to be mere jumbles of human bones.

'But they do not appear to have any heads,' I said to the Great Sitt, 'and there are spare skulls, without bodies.' It was quite true: dotted about in a macabre way were caches of skulls alone amongst the headless skeletons. What had happened to the townsmen? We can deduce something of the course of events of those far-off days from the dry mud and bones that have been left to us. The dead were buried in shallow graves and then a new town wall was built high up round the mound: the suburb was forgotten. This makes us think that perhaps after all, it *was* attack, since the first actions of the survivors was to build an encircling wall, and only later did they have the heart to level up the area where lay the dead, and above them build their houses. But before they built their new homes after the disaster there was one further need. It was a need for skulls (as we shall see later), and so they rummaged among the graves and took many of the heads. Sometimes their rummaging took them through a pit in which two or three bodies had originally been placed. They pulled and pushed aside the decaying flesh; often an arm or leg was entirely pulled away, and sometimes the searching hands disturbed the bones completely. But there is evidence of respect, certain bones have been replaced with care: a leg by a leg, albeit the wrong way up.

They had little or no need of the lower jaw, and so we find the lower jaw replaced in the graves while the craniums are missing. It must have been a ghoulish business but had been carried through relentlessly; the majority of the burial groups had been robbed in this strange fashion. It must have been some one person's task to wrench off the lower jaws as the others fossicked in the pits, and he must have laid the 'finished' skulls to one side as he moved from pit to pit. And then, when the whole work was over, they gathered up the skulls carelessly, leaving here and there a few neatly piled groups

of craniums, which were buried by the builders who came
after them.

New houses: there they are in the section of our Great
Cutting. They were built in the same traditional style,
with the same type of brick and plastered floors. The
years passed by and these houses, too, fell into decay.
But before they were destroyed all manner of rubbish
was discarded, and in it were some of the skulls which
had been so carefully garnered. For two generations or
more these heads must have been kept as family trophies.

We found seven discarded skulls, and, to each, plaster
had been applied and modelled in the semblance of
flesh. In all except one the lower jaw was missing. They
were no longer skulls but works of art. The curve of the
cheek, the pursing of the lips, and the smooth sweep into
the eye socket were most delicately executed. In each
eye socket shells had been embedded to give a semblance
of eyes. In one case cowrie shells had been used, and in
others split fragments of shell had been applied in such a
way as to leave a slit down the middle of the eye which
most vividly gave the impression of a pupil and the gleam
of light that radiates therefrom. Some of these heads still
bore the traces of paint. I think the best way of describing
them, although I must not for a moment underrate their
beauty or Marino Marini's skill, is to say that they resemble those olive-coloured, smug and dyspeptic gentlemen whom Marini is so fond of modelling.

Up to recent times skulls have been so treated in New
Guinea. There we find that they are plastered and modelled as portrait heads, and are placed high above the
houses. Sometimes it is the head of an ancestor and the
motive is one of veneration; sometimes the head of an
enemy is preserved, and again placed high so that all
may see and gloat upon the trophy.

The analogy unfortunately still leaves us with a doubt:
were the heads from our town the skulls of slain Jerichoans preserved for veneration or were they those of
their enemies?

Although it is tempting to assume that there had been
a massacre which would account for the great number of

dead, no signs of violence are visible on the bones. Disease it may have been – but why the sudden rebuilding of the walls? Let us simply call it disaster. And then the calamity and the buried trophies were forgotten as the busy life of the little town surged on. We see that later houses were built and fell into decay, one upon another. The wall was patched, and at some time even extended beyond the old limit. One would have thought that the pattern of life was fixed for another thousand years. But no. At long last, for no apparent reason, our Pre-pottery Neolithic people vanish from the mound and from our story.

Theirs had been a wonderful innings. Nearly half the accumulation of the Tell belongs to their period, which had lasted well over a thousand years.

Who were these people ethnically? We still await the findings of the physical anthropologists, who will tell us wonderful things such as: '... the foregoing analysis thus demonstrates that the variabilities of the physical characters of the two sexes in the ——— series are of the same order, and if there is any difference between them it has not been apparent owing to the small size of the sample. On the whole then, for all practical purposes the series may be considered as homogeneous in regard to its internal consistency'. . . . *Then* we will know all about them. But for the moment a great deal about their lives can be deduced from the material remains they have left to us.

Even when there was no disaster, the people who lived in this very early Jericho had the quaint custom of burying their dead beneath the floor boards. Actually they were not floor boards but, as I have said, the most beautifully burnished plaster floors; and they were a delight to excavate because the accumulated earth and débris above them slithered off so neatly and cleanly under the trowel. If one were lucky a whole section of floor could be exposed intact, and the greyish-white burnished plaster curved gently up to face the room wall. We are not so vastly up to date with our curved floor angles. The housewives of seven thousand years ago in

Jericho could sweep and dust charmingly proportioned rooms designed for labour-saving.

As they reached these levels in the various trenches, the site supervisors became inordinately proud of their plastered floors. In fact from time to time one was captured by the most enthusiastic people on the dig to 'Come and see my plastered floor'.

I remember how on one occasion, days after my first tour of the Tell with the Great Sitt, Charles spotted me as I was plodding past with my drawing board and haversack. He had been a little late in finding his first floor and was making up with extra enthusiasm for what he had lacked during the more dreary days when he had had no floor and many of the others had.

'Come and see my plastered floor,' he called up from what appeared to me a long way down.

It was late in the afternoon, when one does not receive these suggestions with the same gusto as in the morning. I came to the edge of his cutting.

'It is a lovely floor, Charles, one of the best,' I shouted back.

'But you can't see it from there; you must come down.'

'Must I?' trembled on my lips; nevertheless I dutifully made my way to the top of his perilous little staircase and began struggling down between the basket boys – down, down, round the corner where the step was crumbling, up and over two or three walls, down again into a trial trench, and at last came to a halt beside the triumphant Charles.

He was busy demonstrating the beauty and perfection of his particular plaster floor. I suddenly felt I was at the Ideal Home Exhibition and that this really was the very latest thing. How wonderfully it swept up – with two neat swishes he exposed a gleaming surface. Feel it – wasn't the texture beautiful? I restrained myself from saying 'How much a yard?'

'Lovely,' I murmured.

'Here's a bit you can keep,' he said. So I had my sample! There were two or three fragments that had been broken and one of these was proffered. All base thoughts must vanish in the face of such exuberance.

These beautiful floors and walls belonged to houses clustered fairly closely together. Sometimes they were built round courtyards, and the doorways were wide and rounded at the edges. It had been obviously a period of prosperity, and rebuilding had occurred frequently. In all, we worked through nine main building phases, and there were many incidental patchings and enlargings. You must imagine these early town dwellers living closely together, not unlike the modern Arab villager who still packs his small mud-brick house cheek by jowl with that of his neighbour.

In these houses a number of their personal goods have come to light. Most numerous of all are their flint tools. These are delicately shaped knives, scrapers, points and arrow heads. Our townsmen hunted with their bows and arrows, and not in vain. Many bones of gazelle have been recovered from the rubbish pits of the town, and the hunters must have eaten well. Goats, too, are represented in these pits, and may already have been herded – the beginnings of pastoralism. One goat's bone had been so deformed by arthritis that the animal could scarcely have protected itself in a wild state and must surely have lived, crippled, in the security of a tended herd.

More certain, however, than this rudimentary pastoralism was the cultivation of wheat and barley, which were reaped with flint sickles. These sickles are particularly delightful because the constant friction between blade and grain stalk has given a lustre to the cutting

B

edge that remains like a beautiful French polish to this day.

We must imagine the town surrounded by the green fields of the oasis – fields that provided food for about three thousand people. Surely this presupposes an organized system of irrigation? As we have seen, from the earliest times the rulers of Jericho had been able to mobilize communal effort for major works such as the construction of the town wall. The considerable task of cutting and maintaining water channels must equally have been within their scope.

I have already told you of one of the communal buildings, which, we think, may have been a Temple. We found another ceremonial building farther to the north of the town. It was a small rectangular apartment which had been constructed out of an earlier room, and all the doorways were mysteriously blocked: walls and blocking, alike, had been covered with plaster. At the far end of the room a shaped column of volcanic rock fitted neatly into a central niche cut into the wall. The column rested on a rough stone pedestal.

How this sealed room had been used we cannot say, but it had obviously been designed for some ceremonial purpose.

Most of the domestic utensils of our Jerichoans have, unfortunately, vanished with the years. Since they lived before man's wonderful invention of pottery, more than likely they used skins for water carrying and storage, and wood for bowls and platters. There are many stone objects: well-ground bowls and dishes, and innumerable querns for grinding grain. We have found, too, the smooth and rounded rubbing stones that must have been employed upon the querns.

We know that the houses were furnished with mats. In one of the trenches on the plaster floors two or three mats have been found *in situ*. They are about three and a half feet by two and a half feet and were made by binding reeds round and round into an oval shape in what is possibly best described as a raffia-work technique. These mats, and others larger, have survived because they were discarded and covered with protecting débris,

and in their disintegration formed 'ghost mats' of a
finer and more compact substance. As we look at them
today it is even possible to see the binding stitches that
held the reeds together. And one mat bears the tell-tale
track of a white ant who ate his way across it some seven
thousand years ago.

Our early Jerichoans had their art. At first it was only a
glimmering. There is the small carved bone button,
somewhat like a stylized gargoyle; an engraved swastika
in clay and, of course, a 'mother goddess'. She is a tiny
unbaked clay figurine of breasts and waist and hips – a
pathetic little creature really, but a recognizable female
form.

But later, the tragedy of the 'disaster' was an inspiration. In their struggle to immortalize the skulls, as
modelled portrait heads, our ancient artists achieved an
expression at once simple, dignified and strong. With
these heads they raised themselves once and for all to the
level of artists. And since, today, we can trace a continuity of settled life that leads back to them, we must
place them at the head of that line of artists who have
continually struggled for expression, from their days
until our own.

As often happens on excavations, the stupendous finds
tend to come in the last few days. And so it was with the
plastered skulls. The tempo of the dig was at fever pitch,
everyone desperately about his own business polishing
off this and that. The Camp House was being packed up,
the great crates were being filled with 'finds'; bustle and
confusion – no, no, never confusion – everywhere. Into
this busy scene Peter, our stalwart, steady Peter, throws
the squib. He has just discovered some new and wonderful plastered skulls.

Here, alas, I cannot go on. This all happened the season
before I went to Jericho, and I can only indicate what I
have been told of the trials of the few who stayed on to
excavate those heads. The 'dig' packed up all round them
and they squatted on the bare boards of the deserted
Camp House. In the daytime they worked with pen-
knives and paintbrushes loosening the earth from these

unique finds – for unique they are. In all, they unearthed seven. They probed for more; but that was all.

I feel rather strongly over this episode. Somehow all
through my first season there appeared to be a harking
back. 'Ah, you should have been here when we discovered the plastered skulls.' You will admit that this
lofty attitude is infuriating. But I did exactly the same
myself the following season. Perhaps it is a trial which all
'freshers' have to put up with.

When we were working on the Neolithic levels above
the massed skeletons, everyone was content and busy
excavating and recording plastered floors. Oliver, the
surveyor, had planned them all. Nancy, the photographer,
had performed miracles of acrobatics in her attempt to
get the perfect angle to show up such and such a feature.
At last we could proceed to destroy and shovel away, in
order to get to the layers beneath. The pickmen and
basket boys came to life: they love a really good bit of
destruction. I think everyone finds it fascinating to
leave one phase and push on into the unknown. There is
an anticipatory air, and this time no one was disappointed.
There were skeletons below the floors.

Gold possibly ranks highest, but skeletons are magnificent news value. And of course they stand (or lie)
alone in the eye of trippers.

Trippers are simple souls and not unlovable. I remember one absurd occasion when we were working in the
Great Trench on some of these sub-floor skeletons, when
a voice from above bellowed 'Hi-ya'. The owner of the
voice was large and portly, wore no coat and had a tie
with a lobster crawling up it. He was accompanied by his
lady and two friends.

'Have you got old Joshua down there?'

'No,' we explained. 'We are working in the débris of a
considerably earlier period.'

'Don't bother,' he called back. 'Are those Joshua's
walls? Would you throw me up a bit of stone that old
Joshua might have seen? They'd love it back home.'

Suddenly we were overcome with a feeling of help-
lessness. There was an official guide, but either the guide

had not done his stuff or the gentleman with the lobster
had failed to assimilate. But the real crux of the matter
was – 'They'd appreciate it back home.' So we instructed
one of the workmen to pick up a small stone near the
wall and take it up. This was somewhat unprincipled,
I will grant you, but there are times when it is far
better to capitulate immediately than to show fight.
We sensed our gentleman's limitations and gave him
his stone.

Jemil, near the wall, picked one up and threw it to
Ahmed near the stairs. Ahmed took it up and received
a dollar for his pains. Poor Jemil was distraught; he
demanded half the booty, which, naturally, was refused.
The stage was now set for a spirited contretemps and I
cannot think how all this would have ended if our simple
down-to-earth lobster had not produced another dollar.
It dropped like dew from heaven at Jemil's feet, bringing
with it peace.

My partner over these first groups of skeletons was our
delightful American, Todd. I think he suffered sometimes
when he heard the inevitable 'Hi-ya' called to us from
above. We, the Britons, could afford to take a tolerant
and lofty attitude with regard to the swarms of visitors
who invaded our precincts, because our tourist agencies
do not appear to be so enterprising – or is it £ s. d.? Car
loads from Balham are not known to clutter up the road
by the Spring, and whenever we see a fleet, line ahead,
of Cadillacs, we know that Oswego or Illinois is *doing* the
Holy Land. Sometimes we get as many as eighty visitors
in one dose; their delight is to take ciné pictures of us as
we work. I usually draw, bent double over my board,
with the lower edge of the board resting on my toes and
the upper edge against my knees. This has the advantage
of leaving one's arms completely free for measuring, and
the disadvantage that the blood runs to the head when
actually drawing. I found that I was usually caught rear-
view in this attitude by ciné-minded Cincinnati or New
Orleans. Todd, who is one of those incredibly long fellows,
had the art of folding himself up like a camel beside the
skeletons. With his monstrous walrus moustache he was

a sure target for thirty seconds whirring from the cameras.

Slowly we unearthed our groups of skeletons, and two or three very interesting features emerged. Not only had the skulls been robbed from the dead as they lay in their burial pits, and the lower jaws thrown back, but not all the bodies were complete, although there were no signs of violence. One explanation may be that after death they had been allowed to disintegrate to a certain extent before burial. The ligaments had obviously held to keep the articulated portions of the body intact, but certain ligaments had broken and so some of the bodies were minus limbs, or else we found articulated stray limbs. Were they deliberately pulled apart? No one knows.

We gave the various groups names. There was the 'Leggery' which speaks for itself; and the 'Bonery', which was our very first name, as I am sure you could tell from its lack of inspiration. But as a matter of fact it was fairly rightly named because there were not many articulated limbs in the Bonery, just stray bones, although we were able to work out that there were four or five individuals all jumbled up together.

There were the Twins, perfect in every way – poor little fellows, aged about ten or twelve.

There was the Double Headed Monster. He was dramatic. We only had him from the waist upwards protruding from the trench walls. He lay on his face with his arms bent up to his chin, but he had two skulls, his own in good articulation with his neck, and a spare.

The Great Sitt summoned anthropological aid from England. These seven-thousand-year-old skeletons were of the utmost importance, and Dr Cornwall was flown from London to show us how to measure and record.

It was very slow work, and the site supervisors kept demanding our attentions. In fact Charles was becoming impatient with the skeletons in his trench. What with the work in the tombs, and nearly everyone on the Tell having by this time his own grim skeleton problem, we, the bone people, became a little harried.

'When are you going to come and remove my skeletons?' became the monotonous question of the day.

David showed tremendous self help. I had postponed measuring and drawing his baby for a day or two, and then lo and behold the pathetic little chap was found one day wrapped up in brown paper on my desk. David could wait no longer and had dug him out intact in a little square of earth. He looked desperately out of context on my desk. He was duly drawn and recorded, and we looked in his earth for anything that might have been buried with him, but there was nothing.

Charles's problem was more severe. He had two or three groups of skeletons, and it was beginning to hold up the work in his trench. Obviously pressure would have to be brought to bear. But if five supervisors began demanding simultaneously, four would inevitably have to be disappointed. In due course we announced to Charles that we were coming.

'Excellent,' he responded. 'I'm afraid I didn't wait for you. I have gone down all round and I've left you on a bit of a pillar.' I had wondered why he had dropped out of the pressure group; in fact for the last day or two he had appeared almost unconcerned.

His 'pillar' was on the edge of a twenty-foot drop into the old German excavation trench, and on the other three sides he had dug down about six feet all round us. It was quite a job to get on to the pillar, which consisted entirely of a melange of bones. I really forget now whether he left us a step to get up by or whether he expected us to levitate and descend gently among the skeletons.

For five days we worked away at this group, sorting them out, and the first two or three days were not noticeably comfortable. We had nowhere to put our feet or my drawing board or Dr Kurth's excavation tools. Dr Kurth is a German anthropologist from Göttingen and he came to work with us on this early skeletal material.

I do not know if you have ever been perched on an earth pillar covered with skeletons, together with a German anthropologist, for any length of time. It is an interesting experience; and it was delightful to see how we both adapted ourselves to each other and to the circumstances. Dr Kurth's enthusiasm for all our bones was

tremendous. Evidently there are not so many skeletons
of approximately seven thousand years of age, and here
he found himself surrounded with them. This really was
an anthropologist's dream come true. His eyes sparkled,
he never ceased to work, *but* – I suppose there is always a
but – he had his problems on the pillar, and so had I.
He yearned over every single skeleton we had on the site.
'What was happening in the Chalcolithic tomb at this
moment, nicht wahr?' 'And that group of David's,
nicht wahr?' 'And there are all tombs, – ja, ja,' and he
would fix me with an eye worthy of the Ancient Mariner.
He would then beat his forehead twice with a fist and
say 'Tso – to vorrk.' We had been working. But I
sympathized; he had been visited by a demon and he felt
he had to share his passing gloom. Could I have done so
with the wave of a wand, I would have arrested the
relentless progress of our digging and allowed him oceans
of time to love every skeleton. But this could not be; I
am told that anthropologists, if left to themselves, are
rather like glaciers, and are not actually seen to move.

Obviously, with eighty workmen to keep employed,
we had to dig on, leaving here and there little isolated
pockets of anthropological material awaiting his attention. We would come, Dr Kurth and I, and measure,
excavate, draw and record each bone. Those that we
could preserve, we did, and then the pocket would be
dug away and the excavation would proceed downward in
its normal stratified layers.

My problems on the pillar were of a different order.
They were the Doctor's early days on the dig, those
pillar days, and his English was entirely anthropological.
As you can imagine, conversation had a tendency to slow
up. Interested as I was in the lumps and knobs and skeletal variations of prehistoric man, one must admit that it
is a dry diet for any prolonged length of time.

My task was to make exact scale drawings, and to
write the notes and measurements appropriate to each
and every bone. Dr Kurth's was to deduce the racial
types and to make the pronunciamento upon the group.
Since, as I say, the pillar group was a melange, this was

quite difficult. In fact, from a cursory glance it would have been impossible to say what was there except that there appeared to be the pulled-about and half-articulated remains of a number of skeletons. Eventually, with time and patience and much anatomical chatter, our poor little people began to take shape.

But at this stage my problem loomed enormous. I felt that something *must* be done about this one-track conversation – bones. I could not very well say 'Let's work in silence,' because Dr Kurth took it for granted that my life too was dedicated to bones. That I should show him that his partner had clay feet was unthinkable. Every few minutes he would call upon me to admire this 'thickening of the apertura pyriformis', 'this so very interesting widening of the fossa for the sub-lingual gland'. There would be fascinating dissertations on the deductions that could be expected from these discoveries. And we were getting on famously. It was becoming evident that there were the remains of a number of individuals; some were complete and some had been pulled apart, and they had been thrown together into this burial pit.

No, I could never have said to him 'Let us work in silence.' But something had to go. Isolated as we were, down Charles's huge trench, up Charles's ridiculous pillar, with the only bond in common desiccated human bones, I took the decision to make a British compromise. Science would have to give a little. Henceforth our skeletons would lose their scientific names and become personalities. I would rechristen the lot; from henceforth Skeleton A would be known as Freddie, B was Mimi, and so on. It worked like a charm. Dr Kurth took to it quite easily and I was delighted when he would tell me 'Tso, I am now on to Freddie's left tibia. I will give you the measurements. He lies over the calcaneous of Mimi.' You have no idea how gay it all became. We were like a rather select club on the pillar.

In all we had Freddie, Mimi, Bill, Neo-Natus, Agnes, Baby and Fritz. Fritz, I threw in at the end. It suddenly struck me that perhaps I had been too British, and that I

B*

should let him have one German. Fritz was an articulated, crouched skeleton, with an arm missing, right at
the bottom of the group.

I admit I slipped a little over Neo-Natus. If ever there
was a scientific name, there was one. He was very, very
Neo, and consisted of a few friable bones, and a pelvis the
size of a crown piece, and two tiny legs crouched up.
But somehow Neo-Natus suited him. After all, it had a
pleasant classical ring and could almost be a name.
Macaulay might easily have written – 'Out spake Neo-
Natus, a Ramnian proud was he.' But he was the only
concession I made.

Baby and Neo-Natus both had skulls, but of the rest –
Freddie, Mimi, Bill, Agnes and Fritz – the craniums were
missing. This was extraordinarily interesting, because it
put Charles's group into the same category as those in
the Main Trench. The levels were equivalent; the same
plaster floors, the same skeleton groups below floors, and
the same feature that the skulls were mostly missing.

The 'disaster' of which I have spoken had been
extensive. From the evidence we have it seems that
death swept right through our town. The survivors, as
we have seen, rallied themselves, and continued in their
great tradition for some time and then they ceased to
live upon the mound.

CHAPTER THREE

The First Potters

(4500-4000 B.C.)

W E do not know why our first town builders vanished from the Tell. They were followed by folk who had the knowledge of making pottery, who eventually built their houses with an entirely different-shaped mud brick, and did not bother to line their beaten mud floors with the beautiful burnished plaster that the earlier peoples had enjoyed for so long a period.

There is no evidence that any considerable time elapsed between the disappearance of the old people and the incoming of the new. Had there been a barren layer of dust and dissolved mud we could suppose that the town had been deserted and that the weathering of successive winters had laid a pall over the activities of the previous centuries. But there is no such sterile layer: the vestiges left by the newcomers rest directly upon the débris of the old. Here we can only wonder why the earlier folk vanished. Fire, flood and catastrophic earthquakes are the only calamities that leave visible record of their passing. And none of these seems to have affected our town. The old people – the earliest town-builders – vanished; it is tantalizing that we do not know why.

Perhaps, you might say, that in fact they did not vanish at all; that it was *they* who learnt the art of making pottery and merely adopted new ways. But if so, why did they relinquish the art of making such charming floors? Why did they construct their houses with an entirely new type of mud brick? The brick of the first town dwellers was a longish, rectangular affair with thumb impressions all along the axis making a picturesque herring-bone indentation to hold the binding mud.

The new bricks were what we call bun-shaped:
smaller, rounder and minus the jaunty thumb impressions, in fact, just lumps, flat below and bulgy on top. It
is strange that such an inconveniently shaped brick
should have caught the imagination of those far-off
peoples; but evidently it did, because they were used by
builders farther away to the east in the Tigris and
Euphrates valleys at the end of the fourth millennium.
What the connection between our Pottery Neolithic
people and the Sumerian bun-brick builders is, we do not
know. But it is highly improbable that the idea of such
an idiotic brick should have occurred spontaneously to
two different peoples. Somewhere, it may be, there is a
common source for both.

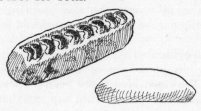

No, for some reason the Pre-pottery Neolithic people
just melted away. It may have been disease, but then
again there would have been more skeletons associated
with the very last layer. They may have got tired of the
old Rift Valley and followed a new leader to a kinder
terrain. We do not know.

We made valiant efforts to conserve both these types of
brick. As they were dug out the difference in temperature
and humidity caused them to dry and crumble. In the
Conservation Department I remember long-suffering
Cecil being surrounded with dozens of them. She tried all
sorts of methods and none of them was altogether satisfactory.

When preserving anything friable, the idea is to get
the object to absorb a strengthening substance. This can
only be done if the strengthening material is in a penetrating solution; so we usually have a plastic (the streng-
thener) in solution with something which has penetrating

qualities. The penetrator is supplied by a spirit: in Jordan we use alcohol.

Cecil, in her den, had tanks full of this mixture and lowered mud bricks gently into them. The result, of course, was bigger and better mud pies. She tried painting the bricks with many doses of a fairly weak solution, but the ultimate result here was a mere penetration of possibly a quarter of an inch, making a pleasant little firm jacket all round the brick. This, of course, would be quite all right provided the brick were on a glass shelf in the loving care of some museum and never moved again. In fact, many of our 'finds', not only bricks, would stand a chance if they could be miraculously transported to glass shelves; but Cecil's was the onerous task of being responsible for their transit. The coated bricks had a horrid tendency to drop in half, revealing their untreated friable innards. She feels now, after some considerable experience, that the best way would be to bake them gently in a kiln – not enough to alter their colour, but enough to 'fix' them. Inscribed tablets of unbaked clay, such as are found abundantly in the ancient cities of Mesopotamia, are normally treated in this way.

But, to return to the ancient newcomers on the Tell, theirs was a tentative beginning. There is evidence that they 'squatted' on the remains of the old town. Hearths are found placed in a haphazard manner among the ruins, and here and there are pits dug down into the old Pre-pottery levels and filled with stony rubble and sherds of the new pottery. There do not appear to be many buildings. The squatters actually squatted. Yet, as I say, they dug pits and many of these are of the most peculiar shape, bulging out below a small mouth. The Great Sitt suggests that they may have been dug as quarries for material for the brick makers. The earth was dumped round the mouth of the hole, and as the quarriers went down it was far easier, if somewhat dangerous, to extend the pit sideways than to remove the dumps. We have not, as yet, found a squashed skeleton in any of these holes so presumably the overhang did not often collapse. But certainly the ancient diggers were tempting Providence.

The technique of mud-brick making as I have seen it
in Jordan today is very simple, and more than likely it
has not changed in all the centuries. The women cluster
together and dig little holes in suitable earth. Others
with sieves separate the finer earth from the rubble,
while Grandmama, who usually directs the proceedings,
pours water from earthenware vessels into the middle of
the fine earth mounds. Leaving a small bank all round
the edge to hold the water, she churns up the mud to
the right consistency until she has obtained a pleasant
scone mixture. Chopped straw is added to act as a binder.
Then the real work begins. Skinny arms are plunged in
and handfuls of glorious mess are ladled out into oblong
wooden moulds, but the moulds have no bottoms and
rest merely upon a board. After a great deal of patting
and pushing the oblong is filled, the containing boards
are lifted, with many a helpful wriggle from round the
'dough', and, with the utmost care, the wet brick is laid
out with regiments of others to dry. After about a fort-
night the bricks are ready for the builder.

The bun-shaped brick of our Pottery Neolithic people
was probably not made in a container, but for the rest the
technique would be the same. Sometimes traces of
chopped straw and even grain, or the impressions of
grain, have been discovered in these early bricks, and
such microscopic finds are, of course, a delight to those
specialists who are working on the subject of early
agriculture. A grain of wheat of 4,000 B.C. tells a tremendous story to those who know. That is the worst of
archaeology – one must miss nothing. Who would have
thought that a grain impression in a mud brick would
help to unravel any mystery?

It is therefore quite probable that these pits were
quarries. And could not the loose rubble, which fills them,
be the rough, unwanted sievings cast back into the hole?
The area was then levelled and buildings were constructed with the bun-shaped bricks.

As the supervisors dig through the various layers, they
have the tricky task of differentiating one stratum or
layer from another. When I told you of the build-up of

the great mud mound, which we call the Tell, I do not think I emphasized the importance of layers. Each layer is the material remains of an episode in the life of the town: it is a page in the history book. The pages must be interpreted in their proper sequence if we are to read the history intelligently.

The supervisors must see that the pickmen understand that it is only the one particular layer that they are to skim off. Then all the potsherds and other 'finds' from that layer are kept together in a basket at the side. The basket is labelled with the name and description of the stratum. In this way the pottery from each phase is kept separate.

For instance, in the diagram on the next page it is possible to deduce that there were five distinct phases. The first, in time, is represented by the layer which we have called 5. Here the newcomers lived on the ground as they found it; they built hearths and broke their pottery vessels. There were wet seasons, storms and mud, and more hearths, picnic litter and pottery. It was all trampled in and formed eventually that most recognizable of all layers: the 'occupation' stratum.

Later their successors dug a pit (No. 4). This is cut through the occupation layer and therefore must be later. We can only guess why they dug it. It may have been a quarry for manure for fields. The accumulated débris of these mounds provides a great fertilizer and has been used over and over again as a top dressing. It may have been dug as a quarry for material with which to make mud bricks. The earth will have been sieved and possibly the unwanted rubble thrown back into the pit; which eventually was filled. Then our Pottery-people decided it was time to build a house, so tremendous scrapings and levellings occurred and the pit and the old occupation surface were buried beneath the levelled earth. This is our Layer 3. The walls of the house and its smoothed mud floor were constructed: Layer 2, and on the floor we find another accumulation, that of a most untidy family: sherds, bones and junk. This is shown in the diagram as Layer 1.

Now if all went well with the supervisor there would be five baskets labelled approximately thus:

Layer 1: Accumulation on Floor.
Layer 2: Floor.
Layer 3: 'Grey fill' (the levelling).
Layer 4: Contents of pit.
Layer 5: Occupation débris.

Some of the baskets may have nothing in them at all. It is not likely that there was much to be found in the purely constructional Layer 2 The Floor, whereas 1, 4

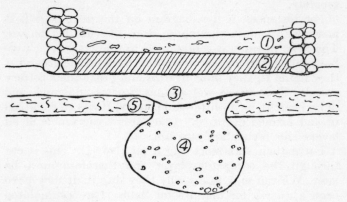

and 5 may have been quite fruitful. I know we are digging for history and we ought to be both keen and calm whatever the layer; but I can assure you that it is far more exhilarating to be digging in a productive layer. Each spadeful is a gamble. Whereas the barren layers, though highly necessary, lack the sparkle of immediate reward.

Everything is labelled. Labels are stuck into the earth section with appropriate number and description: the number and description, as I have said, is written on a label for each basket; and finally a record of the layer, with number and description, is kept in the supervisor's notebook. There has been a snow-storm of labels.

And then what? A measured drawing is made of the

side of the cutting so that we have a permanent record of this tiny portion of the Tell. But it is not isolated from what has gone before, or from what is to come after. It has been drawn in relation to a certain fixed point -- a surveyor's mark on the concrete wall of the Spring, so that each portion of the vertical section, as it is drawn, can be fitted in with what has gone before.

The baskets are taken away in the evening when we all leave the Tell, and are handed over to Dorothy, who presides in the pottery and records room.

She has two wonderful slaves, Suleiman and Moussa. Suleiman is gay, smiling, helpful and energetic, and Moussa is dour and slow. Together they sit all day washing pottery. They have other humble and unmentionable little tasks about the Camp House and some of our Jericho scallywags jeer at them. But Dorothy smooths their path by telling them that theirs is a noble duty – that the comfort of the whole camp depends upon their solemn daily journey to the refuse pit.

Dorothy, too, has other tasks besides those of the pottery room. At ten o'clock each morning she is to be found in a passage that is the laundry, bathroom and infirmary, and she holds the sick parade. All the workmen with ailments present themselves to her. They wait patiently in the passage and, one by one, they sit in the chair of honour in front of the box of medicines. Near them the washerwoman Fatima is crouched over a huge tin bowl, washing innumerable dusty shirts and underclothes. Two Primuses keep up a pleasant hiss, and steam billows along the passage from the kerosene tins of simmering water. Dorothy bends over her patient with an enigmatic expression and takes his slip of paper from him. We have found from long experience that these written recommendations are essential. No workman now can present himself at sick parade without first obtaining a recommendation from his site supervisor. It is the supervisor's onerous responsibility to judge whether the headache, tummyache, backache or constipation is indeed serious. Easy things, like boils and cuts, speak for themselves; but aches become a menace and, before the days of recommendation, lines and lines of addicts would queue up for aspirin until it became a racket. So Dorothy remains sphinx-like until she reads the slip.

'Jemil may have a stomachache. He's obviously under the weather. Suggest something strong.' It is not much to go by but at least it shows that Jemil is bona fide. Information is then elicited from the sufferer. 'Batni bouj'h' which, being translated, means 'stomach pain'. Here, Dorothy has a choice of two alternatives: constipation pills, or 'Gyppy Tummy' pills – usually it is the latter; but now she has developed a sixth sense that directs her to the right bottle. Hard-hearted supervisors have been known to send little notices which read: 'Mahmoud is becoming an absolute menace. Please give him an outsize dose of castor oil.' Through all this tricky diagnosis, Dorothy must find a way and act with assurance. She lances boils the size of golf balls, and bathes feet as tough and horny as a turtle's. One morning a scamp joined in the queue and when she read his proffered ticket: 'Give aspins', he grinned and held out his hand. The childish writing could not have come from any of the team up on the Tell: she knew he had written it himself and so he was bundled out. Very rarely do any of them get badly sick; if they do, we take them to the hospital in the Refugee Village where an overworked and harassed doctor prescribes. The patience and sang-froid of these workmen are quite amazing. Boils, perhaps, are their most painful affliction, and they will not flinch or murmur throughout the entire proceeding. Their gratitude is simple and direct. Occasionally a small and crumpled piece of embroidery, sewn by the man's wife, is rummaged from the pocket and offered to Dorothy in return for all that she has done. They have great faith in Sitt Dorothy's ministrations.

All through this sick parade Fatima washes. One by one the kerosene tins are emptied, to be filled again at the Spring. Her strength must be colossal: this daily wash takes hours and she squats in the passage with her great arms rubbing, and beams upon the world. She is the first wife of a tiresome old refugee; but she bore him no children. She was a failure! He took another – a sprightlier, younger, westernized young woman. No sooner was the second wife in the family-way than Fatima, too, began. Now Papa has ten children, all under six, and Fatima must work to support the family. He has been known to come to the pay parade to receive her wages but the Great Sitt firmly hands them to Fatima herself. What happens subsequently can be none of our business, but we fear the worst.

To return to the Tell. Work ceases at 4.30, when the head foreman blows his whistle. The tools are gathered up, and clutching hands relieve one of all paraphernalia. Like young monkeys, the basket boys swarm up the earthen stairways to the surface carrying drawing boards, survey-poles and haversacks. One by one we emerge from our holes and fall into the procession as it makes its way along the top of the Tell to the one and only gate which leads to the road, and to the house by the Spring. The Great Sitt had to wire the mound to obtain some sort of privacy for the excavations. As we march along, the evening light is exquisite across the valley: the Mountains of Moab are dappled with the slanting rays of the sun. Beyond the vivid green of the oasis, the pink desert stretches down to the Jordan and the Dead Sea. Often, spontaneously, I have turned to my Arab neighbours in that evening procession and exclaimed 'How lovely it all is!' And, as often, they have laughed and thought me simple. How can a desert be beautiful?

All eighty of us push through the mêlée at the Spring: it is just the hour when the women from the Refugee Villages come for their evening supply of water. There are those coming, with the earthenware pots lying sideways on their heads, and those going, with the heavy vessels filled with water, standing upright above them. The action gives them a wonderful carriage. Gathered together there at the fountain, it is possible to see the traditional costumes of many of the districts of Palestine, because they are refugees, herded together now in the new vast camp-towns clustered round the modern

Jericho. The little girls have little pots, and the women
from the Bedouin encampment nearby come with goat
skins slung on donkeys, or even on their backs, supported
by bands round their foreheads. They all leave the pool
dripping and chattering. Occasionally there is tragedy –
a small girl slips and her pot crashes to the ground. The
weeping is uncontrolled.

Through this busy, colourful scene we push our way.
The workmen pile their tools in ranks along Dorothy's
wall; the baskets of sherds are stacked beneath the pottery
tables. The urchins with my board and haversack pene-
trate to the conservation room where I have a desk, and
neatly put them down; and then the men and boys all
make for the stream, and, alongside the half-heartedly
veiled women, splash the water over dusty legs and arms,
heads, necks and ears. We, too, at a little private channel
on the other side of the Camp House, wash hands only
and plod up on to the wall and into the mess-room for
tea. There is silence for a little while we drink and par-
take of more bread and Substance – it will be pleasant
next year when we shall have butter. There is Marmite,
an extraordinary local jam (they don't understand jam
in Jordan), and delicious home-brewed marmalade.
Marmite is the favourite; if one is late, one can just scrape
a little from the empty bottle; if one is very late there is
none left at all. We all slump a little and there is a
noticeable tendency to hook ourselves on to the table by
our elbows. But tea is a wonderful revivifier, and in no
time a provocative remark can stir the company into
argumentative action. That means we are no longer tired
but ready for anything. The more heated the argument,
the happier we all become.

After tea the previous day's washed pottery sherds are
examined. This is a very solemn ritual. The contents of
all the baskets are tipped in little separate heaps on two
huge rush mats. Each small heap has its label. And the
Great Sitt picks out the interesting bits to be drawn and,
for the rest, notes what types of sherds come from each
layer. She is surrounded by a group of us: those who wish
to learn about this strange art of recognizing potsherds –

students who feel it their duty to learn and the earnest members who miss nothing.

Here I must explain about potsherds: they are irritatingly important. *So* much can be told from them and they are *so* difficult to master.

Let us suppose that Ningal, the beloved wife of Umtampt, begins making pots. She uses a particular mixture, shape and decoration. She teaches all the other potters in the town, and the pattern is settled. The generations that follow modify the shape, still later they introduce new designs, they improve the texture, but throughout there is a continuity.

We all know cars and can say, 'Look at that old veteran!' as Geneviève rattles past. Why do we know them? – because we have seen them develop under our eyes from imitation carriages into streamlined fish. The specialist can say that that particular model is an Austin 1934; its fashioning proclaims it as an Austin 1934; and so it is with pottery. Once the sequence has been built up with keen observance from occupation layers, and from comparison with layers at other sites, pottery provides an important time-scale. Even if brand-new types occur, the question is, with what are they associated? What do we know from other sites of any of these types?

It is simple in theory. Practice, I must admit, not quite so easy.

As we crouch over these little heaps at Jericho, and the Great Sitt says 'Now who will tell me about this lot?' I gaze at it and think: 'Oh dear, I have been told – gritty, pinkish, dark-painted bands – how loathsome it looks – I *should* know.' I venture a period – wrong; and so it goes on. But in time we improve and learn the art.

The sherds of our Pottery Neolithic levels are quite distinctive. From the earliest layers very highly developed fine ware is found alongside a coarse ware. The fine sherds come from pots that look something like this in shape (next page), but since all the vessels are handmade, there is great individuality in each. A typical pot had a long broad neck, slight shoulder and handles below the shoulder line. The distinctive decoration is quite elaborate. The early potters covered the vessel with a cream slip then applied a red paint which they burnished to a gleaming finish; the cream slip shines through and makes the pattern. The designs are usually based on a chevron motive and are bold and attractive.

The coarse sherds resemble bits of blackened oatcake. But even so, they are distinctive of their period. When these huge storage pots (the oatcake sherds come from storage jars) were made, the potter added chaff and smoothed the inside of the jar by rubbing handfuls of grass round and round. Then the pots were fired. We

have learnt to recognize the traces of the smoothing grass on the back of any sherd of this group. The texture of the oatcake sherd is repeated by later potters, but it was only the Neolithic people who used the grass-smoothing technique.

We don't know as yet where pottery was invented. More than likely independent developments took place, since any patch of clay, unintentionally chosen as a hearth, will harden when a fire is built over it. In the earlier Pre-pottery Neolithic level, the scorched basin in the Temple floor may have helped to suggest the notion of making fired clay pots. And at Jarmo, up in the Kurdish foothills, Pre-pottery Period pits are found that have been lined with clay and fired. Here at Jericho our pot-makers arrived with a fairly highly developed technique, as shown by their fine burnished ware, which implies an earlier origin elsewhere.

The people who made and used these vessels do not appear to have defended themselves on the Tell with an encircling wall. Presumably they were at peace with the world about them. The remains of their houses lie super-imposed – one upon the levelled débris of another – leaving evidence that their stay was of some duration.

Apart from their pottery they are dull folk. Like their predecessors, they used delicately chipped flint tools, but there is a difference. The fine serrated edge of the earlier sickle blade has vanished; our Pottery-people chipped a coarser flake.

Dull folk – I cannot raise a glimmer of enthusiasm for these people. They have left us too little. Perhaps they led a carefree existence inside their uninspired little houses built of bun-shaped bricks. They may have sung and danced, and enjoyed the transient things of life. I tolerate them because they did not build a wall; they were friends with all the world. But I dislike them because I cannot know them. They are merely the people who brought pottery to our town.

And then they, too, vanished. Perhaps they got bored and drifted away. Anyway, they left their village by the Spring (I cannot bring myself to call theirs a town) and silence descended upon the great mound. It was deserted. A thick layer of fine dark grey earth, that had been humus, seals the occupation.

Professor Zeuner, whom you will meet later, has examined this layer and confirms that it is a 'soil level' and that it would have taken something like three hundred years to form. After a rainy season nowadays, the whole Tell is green with weeds; they mature and drop their seeds and shrivel in the scorching heat of the summer. So it must have been, year after year, at the end of the Pottery Neolithic period about five thousand five hundred years ago; at least in certain areas of the Tell. We have not dug deep enough in all our trenches to see if this layer of desertion spreads the length and breadth of the mound.

CHAPTER FOUR

The First Metal Workers

(4000-3000 B.C.)

LET us leave the deserted Tell for a moment and
come to the busy Camp House. I feel I have given
you the impression that we live on bread and
Substance only. This is not so. Each evening at dinner
we have the most excellent roast. Is it goat or camel? I
am assured on the very best authority that it is, in fact,
mutton.

Vivienne is the house-keeper and therefore one of the
most important persons of our small hierarchy. Upon her
depend the good humour and the good work of the whole
party. She sets out each morning in the 'dig' car for the
modern town of Jericho. It is possible to get nearly
everything in the town. There is an up-to-date chemist
and a grocer's store; but all imported articles are very
expensive. When one remembers that everything has to
come to Jordan either by the tedious overland road from
Beirut, or else up the Gulf of Akaba, and then again by a
long and arduous desert route to Jerusalem, Jericho or
Amman, it is wonderful that the prices are not more than
they are.

The day-to-day shopping is done in the bazaar where
there are stalls of all kinds. The vegetables are enormous;
the cabbages the biggest I have ever seen. At the butcher's
counters the corpses are yet warm. No effort is made to
trim the poor beast: ears, eyes, furry face and tail are all
there, and bits are cut off as desired.

Vivienne is our contact with the outside world of Post
Offices, special tooth-paste and buttons. If we need anything that cannot be supplied from the excellent canteen
at the Camp House, it goes on her list. We can, of course,

go shopward ourselves on Sundays. This is the free day. But there is such a variety of extraordinarily interesting things to do on a Sunday that I am afraid we burden Vivienne unmercifully with our day-to-day wants.

After the pottery session at about six o'clock, a general attempt is made to wash. Even when there is no dust storm we all look like ragamuffins. And those of us who have been burrowing about in tombs, or have been on the windward side of a dump, are covered with a fine film of grey powder. Each has his own method of ablution. I used to fall into line with those who preferred hot water, enough to fill a basin, tucked away behind a sheet in a draughty passage. But, once I had been initiated into the alternative, I preferred to put on a bathing suit, and, whatever the weather, to wallow under one of the water-falls in the channels that lead from the Spring.

We are looked upon as Spartans by some of the hot-water brigade, but we are not as hearty as they think, although we certainly appear to be the sort of people who would break the ice on the Serpentine. It is usually dusk, and possibly a fairly chilly breeze is blowing as we make our furtive way past Mohammedan eyes to our secret waterfalls. But once in and under water, it is not too terrible, for the Spring bubbles up from the earth at 68° Fahrenheit. The fireflies dart here and there among the reeds and the waterfall pounds us in a friendly manner. It is not every night that we emerge with our teeth chattering. The freshwater crabs which cling to the sides of the channel are a complication; nevertheless we get used to them.

But, whichever way we choose to wash, I will agree, it *is* an effort.

Then up into the mess-room for a drink. How clean and unrecognizable we all look! It is at this stage that we divide into sheep and goats about the wireless. There are those who say: 'Excellent, this must be dance music from Beirut'; others who exclaim: 'This is diabolical; when can we have a decent concert?' And others again who cannot tolerate the wireless at any time, except possibly for ten minutes to hear the news, in rather original English, emanating from Cyprus. Wirelesses are disturbing things.

Dinner is a pleasantly social meal. Breakfast, lunch and tea tend to be somewhat 'shop', but dinner, with its soup and roast and fruit salad, and its occasional bottle of local wine, is always a conversational surprise. After three months of close proximity, one gets to know one's neighbours pretty well. Yet, at dinner there is always hope. Somebody's great aunt, for example, makes home-brewed wines; here is a new topic – so off we go.

This, too, is the great time for barter. 'I'll do anything for anybody if they will mend my shirt.' These are wonderful opportunities. The poor braves are made to work hard. I remember I had an excellent little dam constructed near my tent, where I could clean my teeth and perform minor ablutions, in exchange for sewing on some buttons. I think I insisted on maintenance of the dam in the same bargain.

In the evenings after dinner a silence falls upon the mess-room. Bridge is a very earnest thing and casts an atmosphere of 'Pray be quiet' about the room. The letter-writers scribble away surrounded with an aura of smug-ness, plunging the non-letter-writers into gloom at the thought of the lines that should be written, but are not. Possibly a Canasta group temerariously breaks the silence from time to time. In the drawing office the good-concert devotees may have achieved their object. They will be found strewn about the floor with that curiously im-mobile expression and glazed eye affected by the good music-listener.

Occasionally we have been known to stroll out into the beautiful, almost tropical night, and we have made our way to the small tables under the bougainvillaea which belong to the up-to-date hotel, where it is possible to buy beer. But this does not occur very often as beer is five shillings a bottle.

There are evenings too when we go to the Dead Sea; these are usually 'special party' evenings. The celebra-tion in honour of Jordan's Independence Day found us there. Mohammed, the young Jordanian member of the team, took charge. He decided that we were to have a party such as we would never forget. A bus was hired from Jericho and into it we bundled: cooks, servants, all of us. The evening was black but starlit, and the pot-holes in the desert track showed up like craters in the headlights. Inside the bus the drumming and the bumps, the singing and the dust reduced us all from earnest archaeologists to basic bean-feasting humanity.

Beside the oily, still water we lit a bonfire which burnt with green and blue flames, because the wood we had gathered was impregnated with strange chemicals from the Sea. And over the flames a sheep was roasted. Many of us bathed in the absurd water that held us like rubber balls upon its surface; and when the moon rose above the Mountains of Moab, the feast was ready and we toasted Jordan. Our workmen from the Tell arrived, to sing and dance in the moonlight. We roared back 'John Peel' (British community singing is a tragedy!) but the soloists saved the day. Dr Cornwall gave us lilting songs from Spain; Todd, folk-songs from America.

Mohammed beamed upon us all. It had been his party – and a wonderful success.

But usually in the work-a-day evenings we find we must 'finish off that little bit of work'. So, tucked away in conservation room, photographic and pottery rooms, there are those who are busy keeping up to date or preparing for the morrow.

Dr Kurth, our German anthropologist, was over-whelmed with material when we discovered the great Chalcolithic tomb. He felt then he could never again join the revellers. But we bullied him a little and made him sing us drinking songs; and we insisted that he did not work *every* Sunday.

I will admit that the Chalcolithic tomb was somewhat overpowering: its floor was tiled with over four hundred skulls.

Chalcolithic means 'copper-(and)-stone'. In Palestine at this period (*c.* 3500 B.C.) small communities were giv-ing up their old nomadic ways and adopting new-fangled ideas. Village-life and pottery had come to stay, and now there was this brilliant new discovery – copper. Each small community developed fast in its own way, and a delightful individuality emerged. Sometimes it is difficult to trace the development from one phase to another; and it is hard to say whether any given spot is late Neolithic or early Chalcolithic. Much more excavation is needed before a clear-cut story can be told of this period. All we know is that the old stone axes and arrow-heads were being replaced by copper ones, and new types of pottery were superseding the established Neolithic.

One of the earliest Chalcolithic settlements may have been on our Tell, as potsherds of the period have been found; but the present expedition has not located the levels. The sherds were dug from the mound and dumped by later town dwellers, and we do not know where the settlement lay.

There are other early sites in the Wadi Ghazzeh in the South of Palestine, and on the Yarmuk river to the North. A definite and striking example of a later flourishing Chalcolithic community has been excavated at Ghassul, only about fifteen miles from Jericho. Here the development is easier to trace. The little town was destroyed by fire some time in the fourth millennium; but before that calamity overtook it, the inhabitants had lived in sturdy, well-constructed houses of mud bricks built on stone foundations, and had painted their walls with remarkable geometric patterns.

Exactly how Jericho will fit into this composite story is not yet clear. So far, the excavations have revealed some of the earliest-looking Chalcolithic material at present known; but its most spectacular contribution is of a later kind, and consists above all of a series of very notable tombs.

These tombs of *c.* 3000 B.C., for all their macabre character, may be described as the liveliest relic of this obscure and remote age. Just now we left Dr Kurth working far into the night upon the records of these burials, so it is time to visit the tombs themselves and to take part in their unearthing.

But first, something must be said as to the place and circumstance of their discovery.

As yet I have told little of the great colony of refugees which sprawls at our doorstep. They are Arabs from beyond the Israelite border, who, within the space of a few hours, found their world had crashed about them and streamed in droves across the frontier. Now here they were, helpless and without hope, the subjects of international charity and quartered *en masse* at this spot for the self-same reason that Jericho itself had stood here: namely, the presence of a perennial spring.

At first they lived in tents supplied by the Relief Committee. But as the years slipped past they have built themselves little houses. There are three great refugee villages based on Jericho, but only one of these comes into our story. It is called Ein es Sultan, after the Spring, and it lies on the arid, desert slope immediately north of the Tell and of the Spring. A military hand has designed the village – it is as regular as a chess board; and along the length of these straight and criss-cross desert spaces, which I suppose must be called streets, the peasant refugees have built their tiny, mud-brick houses.

Each house consists of one room, with a door and an unglazed window, fronted by a small courtyard with high mud walls. There is not a blade of green. All the water for the twenty-two thousand souls of Ein es Sultan village is brought in water-vessels balanced on the heads of the women who go daily to the Spring. Lorries, filling at the Spring, supply the water for the institutions: the hospitals and schools; but the families draw their own. If it is washing-day the women will make as many as four or five journeys to the stream. Their lives cannot have changed so drastically as those of the men. Their tasks go on: grinding corn, fetching water, cooking, sewing and looking after the innumerable children; but the refugee men, alas, have *nothing* to do for the fertile land about is owned by the Jerichoans. They can only wait and hope that some day something may be done for them. Each month the Relief Committee distributes food, stores and clothing, and each day the Committee's sanitary squads comb the village for refuse – sweeping, tidying, burning. They have become great pals of ours, these sanitary fellows, because among their many tasks is that of digging huge trenches for latrines; and it is in the course of this labour that they have tumbled into many a tomb – thereby locating them for us.

It was not known that the ancient burial-grounds swept round on the lower slopes to the north of the Tell. Tombs had been located and dug to the west by former excavators, but the wonderfully rich northern area was only discovered by the refugee latrine-diggers and mud-brick quarries. I know you must be thinking: 'Good heavens, it would appear fairly obvious to put a few trial-pits to the north – anyone could have located those tombs.' But it is not as easy or as obvious as all that.

Finding tombs is quite a business. Fourteen of the excavation's workmen are allocated to Diana, who super-vises the tomb-digging. Fourteen – that means seven pairs consisting of a man and a boy. Each pair sets off to dig a little hole – the man digging, the boy dumping the earth. After the digging and dumping have taken them down through the surface-soil, one foot, two feet or three, they will strike the natural rock. Their hopes, all our hopes, are dashed. They fill up their little hole and pro-ceed to start again. If, on the other hand, they do not strike the natural limestone, but continue burrowing down, then it is fairly certain that they are in the en-trance-shaft of a tomb, or even into a great 'open' tomb itself. The excitement is tremendous, of course, once they have dug down a little way and there is hope that it is a shaft. They then begin digging sideways to locate the wall, and perhaps they will come across a sherd of pottery, which gives a clue to the date of the infill of the shaft, and thus, a hint towards the period of the tomb.

The graves are clustered together in little groups and there can be a long and barren search before a new group is located. So you can realize how helpful the latrine-diggers are.

They run to us breathless: 'A tomb, Sitt, a tomb. Come now.'

Paradoxically enough, the village which showed us the way to the new and fruitful tomb areas is now our greatest hindrance. Small permanent homes block the way to so much history and treasure. Nevertheless, we have probed the vacant areas and found much that is very valuable in so doing.

On the Tell we dig for history. We unravel the story of man's endeavour to develop from the newest of new boys at town-dwelling into sophisticated urban denizens. Each phase is presented to us as a puzzle consisting of broken and discarded remains. We wrest from the Tell the plain, straightforward story. But with the help of the tombs we are able to embellish the story here and there. From the dead, strangely enough, we are given a vivid picture of the living: of their art, the utensils they used, glimpses even of their toilet-requisites, their jewellery, their chairs, stools and tables. In death, one can almost bring them to life, imagine them in their setting, with many of their personal goods about them. And so we dig the tombs to enrich our knowledge of the people who lived so long ago. Certain of the skeletons and bones must be kept for anthropological study; but the rest we gather up and bury again, having learnt their story.

One huge Chalcolithic tomb was located in the side of a dry wadi on the fringe of the Refugee Village. Whenever it is certain that the little exploratory hole is no longer merely the hopeful hole, but in fact a shaft or 'open' tomb, the digging pair concerned become almost broody, and their stature and importance increase relative to the magnificence of the tomb.

The two workmen who dug the Chalcolithic grave are perhaps our pets; although they are all such simple and endearing fellows that it is untrue to say that one is more of a charmer than another.

All the tomb-diggers are refugees and are a little group apart from the men on the Tell, who are Jerichoans. Inevitably there is an atmosphere of tension and rivalry between the Jerichoans and the refugees. Jericho, never wealthy, found itself swamped with homeless peasants from the hills and the fertile coastal plain. It accepted the situation, but now the guests have outstayed their welcome. To the poor of modern Jericho, the refugees are almost the privileged ones; receiving, as they do, food and clothing regularly once a month. True, they are subjects for sympathy. 'But are we not poor also?' say the local, impoverished labourers. And thus it is that the Great Sitt employs the townsmen for the Tell, and the refugees for the tombs.

Nimr and Rushty were the finders of our Chalcolithic tomb. Nimr is tall, gaunt, picturesque and the finest workman that we have at the tombs; and his lieutenant Rushty is the youngest on the pay-roll. He is eleven. I think he must have been smuggled in when no one was looking, but he is so willing and gay that I know the Great Sitt would not have the heart to dismiss him. He hauls baskets until the blood vessels stand out on his forehead, and swaggers through the village – a man – with a microscopic dagger slung to his belt.

It was *their* tomb, and together they dug it carefully to the very floor, which was lined with skulls.

As soon as a tomb is located, Diana gives it a number and page in her notebook. With this particular grave we instructed Nimr and Rushty to dig first one half and then the other; and they went down carefully, digging with trowels, layer by layer. Each of the upper layers represented a separate burial. First, at the top, we came to the last fellow to be interred. Nimr is a master at uncovering fragile bones and pottery, and with a paintbrush and a penknife he laid bare for us the topmost skeleton. There he was, that ancient Jerichoan, lying on his side enclosed by stones that had been placed boxwise round him, and surrounded by his burial-offerings of jugs and bowls. Diana gave him an index letter – A. Alas poor Yorick, he was only 'A'! And she numbered all the pottery associated with Burial A in Layer 1. I then came and plotted the stones, the skeleton and the pots upon a plan. On my plan I also marked poor Yorick 'A', and I gave my drawn pots the numbers that Diana had given to each, so that her notebook and my plan tallied absolutely. Then Nancy, the photographer, took an overall photograph. The recording was finished, so we lifted him and his pottery from their age-long resting place. Nimr and Rushty dug

The Plates

Hill country above the Jordan Valley
The road down into the Valley

SEA LEVEL

ng: *Jericho, the oldest town walls in the world, c. 6000 B.C.*

The Camp House by the Spring

Human skull with features modelled in mud plaster

Early skeleton from which the skull has been robbed

Moussa and Suleiman washing pottery

'The Great Sitt' working on the potsherds

g: *The Main Trench cut into the ancient city mound*

'Sitt Dorothy'

Charles

Dr Kurth with Nimr and Rushty in the great Chalcolithic Tomb

John the artist and myself
playing Arab drums

Dr Kathleen Kenyon, 'the
Great Sitt'

Admiring throng round an open tomb

Like ancient Jericho: modern Erbil in Iraq

Air photograph of Jericho

Tomb shaft and entrance

Tomb-digging: the spectators arrive

Inside a Middle Bronze Age tomb

Checking a tomb-list in the courtyard

Wooden table, platter and basket in one of the rich tombs

Women at the Spring

The Refugee Village: a Tell in the making

The water channel below the Camp House

David packing

Wooden box shaped like a
pomegranate

Woollen textile

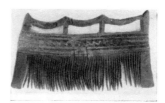

Wooden comb

Wooden platter

on down to the next layer. There were about five or six articulated skeletons buried one above the other, each with accompanying pottery, and each was treated with the same impersonal respect.

By this time we felt we understood the burial practices of those far-off people, and could almost visualize the solemn little ceremony as it must have been enacted on these slopes over five thousand years ago. There would be the procession, winding up the wadi, bearing its burden. A few must have entered the tomb and arranged the stones carefully, placing the body at rest among them. The funeral gifts were put to hand, and then all was covered over with a pall of earth. But no – in this self-same tomb the earlier customs were entirely differ- ent. The lowest of our peaceful burials lay immediately upon a melange of bones and skulls that had been heaped into a common grave. All round the edge of the tomb the skulls had been piled carefully, about three deep. In the middle of the tomb there were skulls too, but they were mixed more freely here with bones. Very occasion- ally we would find an upper arm in articulation with the lower arm, but mostly they were just tumbled bones and skulls.

What were we to think now? Diana's notebook and my plans showed us that we had been through the alphabet over sixteen times. Here were the remains of four hundred and twenty persons. And the fact that certain limbs were in articulation told us that disintegration had not been complete when the bones had been gathered up and packed into the great cavern which had been dug into the side of the wadi. Scattered throughout the pile of bones on the floor of the tomb we found many beads, some of them still lying in position, held by the earth as once they had been held by a thread, and in one instance a bracelet of carnelian beads lay encircling that little nest of bones that had once been a wrist. There were one or two small pots, and that was all.

Had the bodies been exposed until the flesh had rotted away? Had they been buried elsewhere and disinterred to be collected here? These are questions that we cannot

C

answer. But what we do know is that a great number of
skeletons had been gathered together and carefully
packed into the communal grave. The skulls were placed
with the utmost care one upon the other – in most cases
the fragile bones of the nose and face were not crushed or
broken. They must have all been buried together at the
same time. But, I repeat, some limbs were yet held
together by ligaments and must have been brought into
our tomb fairly shortly after death, while others had been
long dead. Why so many buried together with such care
in a single moment of time? If the tomb at this period
had been used and re-used for more and more burials,
the delicate bones of the face would not have survived
such trampling and such movement.

The tomb was roughly oval, with measurements
approximately of fifteen feet by twelve feet; it was a hole
cut into the soft limestone, and the floor lay at a depth of
some eight feet from the surface. Now, unfortunately, we
cannot tell if it had been roofed because natural denuda-
tion of the slope has removed the upper features of the
tomb, whatever they were. And, again unfortunately,
later tomb-diggers had destroyed the entrance.

You can imagine how poor Dr Kurth was overwhelmed with material. The very thought of a game of
Bridge in the evening was sacrilege.

Diana and I were a little overburdened too. By this
time our workmen were digging tombs all over the
Refugee Village, and the physical effort involved in doing
the rounds two and three times a day was quite exhausting. We would make our way from one tomb to another;
recording, drawing, directing. It was not only the com-
plexity of the layers, and the difficulty of measuring, that
weighted our steps when we found ourselves plodding in
the direction of our big Chalcolithic tomb, but we knew
that as soon as we were spotted coming up the wadi the
old watchman would go into his mud house and put on
the Primus prior to offering us refreshment. How un-
gracious all this sounds, but those tiny glasses full of tea
and coffee sometimes became a real trial. Punctilious
etiquette demanded that, once offered, we should accept

these offerings. His kettle was filthy: the soot and grime of years adhered to every portion of it; his glasses were even more filthy, but his heart was of gold. What were we to do but sip the brew, and smack our lips, and gratefully accept a second filling, which is *de rigueur*?

Poor old boy! He lived alone. Nimr told us that he had had five wives. Two were dead and three had run away; so there was no one to clean his kettle, or his glasses!

A watchman is hired for each good tomb or group of tombs. He is usually the householder who lives nearest and his tasks vary from supposedly sitting up all night guarding our treasures, to housing the tools and 'finds', if it is not convenient for us to take them back to the Camp House each evening. We found our old Bluebeard was really quite a pleasant fellow; but then, of course, we had not got to live with him. He squatted like a peculiarly derelict vulture on the edge of the tomb all day – when he was not concocting brews that sickened us – and he housed, on an average, forty skulls a night, all in cardboard boxes packed about his one and only tiny room. We found him most co-operative.

In all, we have had seven of these Chalcolithic tombs. Their finding, fortunately, has been staggered over the seasons so that no one year has been overloaded with more than two, or possibly three, of them. There have been affinities in the pottery and in the style of burial in each. And the pottery types are reflected in the Late Chalcolithic layers and tombs at towns such as Tell en Nasbeh, Ai and Tell Far'ah. This was still the period of hand-made vessels – before the potter's wheel – and so we find the charm of unrestricted exuberant imagination in certain of the forms.

Each evening as we gathered up our treasures and waited for the 'dig' car to come to take us back to the Camp House, Diana could never restrain her enthusiasm for this early stuff: the ridiculous little podgy juglets and the beautiful bowls painted with a linear decoration. It must be enchanting to be a potter.

Each evening the car collects us at some appointed rendezvous in the Refugee Village, and then the perilous journey back to the Camp begins. We all sit clutching 'museum-pieces', and we are packed about with boxes full of bones and pottery. This is the moment for the small boys of the vicinity; but for us the evening torment has begun. Their game is simple and consists of throwing pebbles at the car. Rules are non-existent and a good noisy bang and the sight of our irate faces is reward enough for any amount of waiting. We were foolish enough to think that we could discipline them with a biff or two administered to whomever we could catch; but this did not make the slightest difference, and numbers are against us. So our stately journey home is an irritating affair. We have, perforce, to journey slowly, because of our delicate and valuable burden, and this makes us a sitting target. Even three-year-olds can hardly miss.

You may think that we have accepted this irksome situation too calmly. But even the local police are helpless: apart from boiling a few in oil as examples to the rest (and one never catches the ringleaders), nothing can be done. They gather and scamper away like sparrows in a cornfield, and there are hundreds of them.

But coming and going in the morning, and at lunch-time, is a different story altogether. We are not hampered with a precious load, and we can indulge in a turn of speed and take evasive action. As I say, neither side is restricted by rules, and Diana and I have learnt, when the pursuit is hot, that magnificent results can be expected if one suddenly brakes hard. With any luck a few pile up on the back of the car and knock their demon skulls! This keeps the opposition at a more respectful distance and we are only vulnerable to the accurate long-distance lobber. You must not think that these little boys are any worse than small boys the world over. The Great Sitt was telling us that, when she was digging in Southwark, many a time work nearly came to a standstill because of attentions received from the budding manhood of that distinguished Borough.

At the House we press-gang all and sundry to help unload the car, and our freight is carefully carried through the multitude gathered at the stream at this hour, and safely deposited in allotted store rooms. Here it awaits the attention of those who will wash, register, draw and pack away.

You may wonder how we date all this ancient material. It is all very well to say that this level is later than the one below it, therefore the pots in the lower layer are earlier; but the mind likes to have something more definite than that. It likes to pinpoint man's achievement somewhere in the great record of endeavour.

So, very simply, what has happened is this. Egyptian records take us back to the neighbourhood of 3000 B.C. and dated Egyptian pottery conveniently transfers its date to alien pottery – let us say Palestinian – found with it. Thus we have a date for the associated Palestinian wares. But what of the long ages that preceded the beginning of history? Until recently only a relative sequence could be established in accordance with the relative position of the pottery or 'find' dug from the soil. It was largely guesswork.

But now, since 1949, a revolutionary method of dating remote things has emerged as a by-product of atomic research. This new method is known simply as 'Radio Carbon' or 'Carbon 14' dating. It works roughly as follows. In the carbon dioxide of the atmosphere are to be found two atomic components: radio-active carbon atoms of atomic weight 14 – known for short as C 14 – and 'ordinary' carbon atoms of atomic weight 12 (C 12). The mutual proportion of these atoms in the carbon dioxide of the atmosphere is stable. Plants absorb carbon dioxide, and since all animals derive their body material from plants, C 14 and C 12 are incorporated in all living organic matter. Even the vulture that lives on flesh is absorbing it at second-hand through the body of its prey. But once an organism is *dead* (e.g. when a tree is cut down or a flower pulled up) it ceases to take in carbon from the atmosphere. On the contrary, from the moment of *death* the C 14 content slowly diminishes, and it diminishes at a *known rate*. Now, by the new machinery the surviving proportion of C 14 to C 12, in a particular *dead* organic substance, can be determined, and thereby the time that has elapsed since *death* can be calculated.

It all sounds very easy, but – and there are hundreds of buts – bones are not good subjects: the concentration of C 14 is not really high enough in them for the laboratory tests. Charcoal is excellent. But how often do archaeologists find sufficient quantities of archaic charcoal? Contamination can introduce awkward factors; and so on. Yet in spite of all these difficulties, with improvement in technique, it is hoped that it will be possible to date the *death* of certain ancient organic fragments within two hundred years, either earlier or later, up to a maximum of forty thousand years or more.

So you can see the vast possibilities of C 14 dating. We have found certain scraps of wood and charcoal in our Chalcolithic tomb, but as yet we have not had the results from the laboratory test. These C 14 analyses will now keep the archaeologist in order and will make him think twice before guessing too wildly at the antiquity of his discoveries.

CHAPTER FIVE

The Great Builders

(THE EARLY BRONZE AGE: 3000-2100 B.C.)

THIS was a wonderful period of expansion – the Early Bronze Age. Not only was our own town re-occupied and built up into a sizeable city, but towns and villages in Syria, Palestine and, farther afield, in the great river valleys of the Tigris and Euphrates and the Nile, were organizing themselves into flourishing communities. As we have seen, this was no new experiment at Jericho; already in the Neolithic the site had been fortified, on something more than a village scale, centuries before any similar attempt is known to have been made elsewhere.

But now recognizable cities were to become almost a commonplace. Urbanization was the driving force of the times.

Jericho was again fortified with a stout town-wall enclosing an area of some seven to eight acres. The lure of the Spring and the fertile oasis had once more enticed man into the arid wastes of the Rift Valley.

The idea of towns had spread abroad, much as, earlier, the idea of pottery had spread. It is difficult to point to any particular group of peoples and to say: 'Here was the genius.' Throughout the Near and Middle East, and in the Valley of the Nile, civilization was developing with an impetus that perhaps was lacking in the more isolated and tentative efforts of earlier periods. The Levant and Palestine were keeping well abreast in this great progress. Alas, they were outstripped – not in the art of making towns, for theirs equal the stateliness of their rivals – but in the vital art of writing. The King Lists and other records of Egypt and Sumer are already leading us on into

71

historical times in the river valley civilizations, and there we are able to trace the development of real people.

Our people at Jericho remain shadows cast by the material traces they have left. Trade we know existed between Egypt and Palestine, because pottery typical of the latter has been found in the early Pharaonic tombs at Abydos and Saqqara. But they seem to have resisted the art of writing, which is a pity, because from now on they are thereby doomed to a more lowly place in the story of man's endeavour. We are blinded a little by the recorded achievements of the river kings.

All through the third millennium, then, in Palestine the little towns were becoming walled citadels. At Jericho yet another wall was now built round the old city mound. In the section of our cuttings you can see it built into the sterile band of earth which represents the long period of desolation that elapsed before the newcomers had arrived. Attached to this wall one of our cuttings showed a small semicircular external tower. Only the stone foundations survived the onslaughts of earthquakes and time, but sufficient of it remained to indicate its size and proportion, and it emerged as a monument to the town's enterprise.

The story of the series of walls of this period is a long and complicated one. Some were destroyed by earthquakes and their tumbled remains can be seen in the section on the outer slope of the Tell. Some were destroyed by fire. Others were merely bad walls and needed reinforcing with an outer skin. Then, with another earthquake, they would all collapse, and the builders would have to begin over again.

In our great section, as one looks at this formidable series of walls, one cannot help but feel a little sorry for these valiant town dwellers who suffered so regularly from wall-trouble. In all, over a period of nearly a thousand years, seventeen town-walls were built. Some increased the size of the town a little and some retrenched it. In one way or another, every third or fourth generation must have been confronted with the burden of rebuilding.

Within the walls we can trace the achievement of these people through their houses and their developing pottery forms. In pottery, this period is characterized by a firm hard ware covered with a burnished red slip. The potters became masters at rubbing criss-cross and other patterns on the burnished surface. They loved to make miniature vessels which they buried by the dozen with their dead. The use of the potter's wheel was now beginning; often we find that only the rims have been finished off on a wheel.

We must imagine these people in mud houses of a type which has scarcely altered to this day. In a corner would stand the great heavy cooking-pot, blackened by the fire. There are bowls and burnished platters for the meal. What they did with their ridiculous little juglets I cannot think, because the hole through the neck is often so small that it would require an age to pour a satisfactory tot. They loved storage space: there are urns and bins and crocks built in everywhere.

Peter's area contained a plethora of these Early Bronze Age storage bins. He was obviously digging in the heart of a residential quarter where the good housewives insisted on all the latest gadgets. His maze of houses bristled with built-in etceteras. He became broody – it is a disease supervisors get when they are on to anything new or spectacular. One by one we would be invited to see Peter's clay-lined bins. I remember a day when I was there for the sole purpose of admiring them. The Great Sitt was studying a section with Peter and for a few moments there was silence: bin-loving and concentration were in progress. Suddenly, over the top of the cutting appeared the heads of three men. In the centre the stolid face of our foreman gazed down on us, and on either side were the heads of two local policemen. It must have been tiresome for our poor foreman that he had to be spokesman – the police had no English.

'They have come to take me away,' he informed the Great Sitt.

'Nonsense,' was her reply. 'Tell them that they can't possibly take you away now.' And she entered the fray in the most stirring Arabic.

c*

Much to my delight the little scene was continued in English: I should have hated to miss any of it.

'They say I must come to prison now unless I pay the £3 I owe in taxes and I have not got £3.'

'You can't possibly go now: you are in charge of my eighty men. Tell them to come to the Camp House after tea. I will give them the £3 and it will be docked from your pay.'

To this the police agreed, and our foreman lapsed into Arabic to thank the Great Sitt. No doubt he called her the Dew in the Flower of the Thorn Bush and the Dawn on the Mountain Peak, and other such gracious terms that they employ on these occasions. But I was barred by language from these niceties.

I am afraid it was in more than writing that our Jerichoans failed. True, their pottery developed splendidly, right through the Early Bronze period. They imported and must have appreciated a style we call 'Khirbet Kerak', which is so fine and so beautifully burnished black and red that it is a delight to behold; but they failed in the general development of their art. When one contrasts their artistic achievement with that of the river civilizations, one is left a little sad. There are small figurines of goats and bulls, and we were inordinately pleased to find them. But towards the end of this Age, Egypt and Sumer were well away, and Jericho and Palestine the poor relations.

The tombs that we found of this period are great communal graves. One in particular, I remember, was right in the heart of the Refugee Village in an area to which we gave the imaginative name of Area A. I tell you this because much happened in Area A, and I think you should know it. It was about half a mile into the village and had been left an open space because of the excellence of the compressed sand in the area for brick-making and digging pits for latrines. Here, too, because it was a convenient open space, was constructed the village slaughter block. Unfortunately for us, the tomb team, our ancient Jerichoans had also found that this area had its uses, but for none of the reasons I have just given. It was good for digging tombs. So in this rather Grand Guignol place we found ourselves excavating and recording tomb after tomb after tomb.

One particular Early Bronze grave was tucked away on one side of Area A. The smells, the flies, the little boys all combined to harass us, reaching a crescendo each week with Friday. This is their day of worship, and the day the little boys are not incarcerated in school. We would have perhaps a hundred or more squatting on the edge of the large open hole that was the grave. The scuffling, the pushing and giggling were a constant feature of their presence. Occasionally the prattle became an overpowering roar, and Diana and I were deafened as we tried to work in the tomb.

Our workman here was a go-ahead character called Mohammed. Often he would leap out of the tomb brandishing a long and swishy cane – but there would not be a boy within reach. Like Trafalgar Square pigeons they fluttered away only to come back to roost in a much wider arc round the tomb. Mohammed usually beats the ground two or three times to demonstrate his mounting anger and the potentialities of his stick. He glares at them and swipes furiously at space for a time. He even advances a step or two. The waiting arc widens a little farther. Mohammed returns to the tomb: we all continue work. Slowly, imperceptibly, the small boys cluster in again, silently at first. Then the scuffle and the giggle and the prattle and the roar – and Mohammed is out of the tomb brandishing his stick all over again. Fridays are tiring days: vivid but exhausting.

In this Early Bronze tomb we dug down through layer after layer of successive burials. Some of the bodies may have been exposed elsewhere until the flesh disintegrated and the bones had been gathered up and placed to rest in the communal grave. Some of the skeletons were lying fully articulated. And near each group of bones a cluster of grave goods had been placed. There were a few normal-sized vessels, but the majority were of miniature design and consisted mainly of enchanting little juglets. Some were even as small as two inches in height, with

two tiny handles, one on either side. Beads had been
buried with the dead and strange little pierced animal
bones which we named, naturally, 'cult objects'. For a
long time they puzzle the Great Sitt. What were they?
They were all of the same bone, the metacarpal of a
sheep, goat or gazelle. Three, sometimes two, small holes
had been bored towards one end on the flat surface. And
then at the extreme ends, making an air passage right
through, other holes had been bored. But not in all cases
were these borings present. 'Cult object' was obviously
the word that covered everything. Were they amulets?
Amulet is another good descriptive word that can be
applied to nearly anything. Then someone brilliantly
suggested flutes. It was an attractive thought and held
the field for a day or two until some saboteur pointed out
that the bones without any holes at all would be difficult

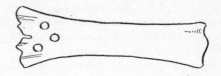

to play. That was quite true, so we were all plunged into
gloom once more until John, our artist, musician and
eccentric-in-chief, was one evening heard producing tiny
mournful noises from the pottery room. He was playing
an Early Bronze Age flute. By inserting two delicate
reeds into the end holes and breathing into them as only
those who play wind-instruments know how to breathe,
he was producing sound. An ethereal Do and an ethereal
Re brought us all full of admiration to the pottery room.
He became emboldened and gave us a performance. Do,
Do, Re, Do – Re, Re, Do, Re, Do. And so on – it was
magnificent. Yet even the most appreciative audience
becomes satiated with only two notes, however sensitively
played, and one by one we drifted away.

But the problem still remained – what about the bones
with no holes at all? Had the relatives of the dead man
popped in unfinished flutes? Since we cannot for certain

say that they are pipes, we cannot convincingly accuse them of this slovenly deed.

Slowly, carefully, the recording, planning and photography progressed. It was a long business. And in Area A one was always working against distractions. One morning I was alone there when a little procession arrived at the neighbouring slaughter block. Small boys ran from all sides to be in time. The poor cow was lowing. Suddenly, with a grip at my heart, I realized what was afoot. I took my measurements with rather a tense deliberation but my eyes seemed to be fixed to the skeleton that I was drawing. 'Oh, that they would be quick,' was my only thought – but the plaintive lowing continued. Then there was a strange gurgle, a few strained long gasps, at last, silence.

It was a solemn moment. Death was with us.

My planning was a little laboured for some minutes, and I was sad. But how horribly resilient we are. Driven by an almost uncontrollable curiosity I lifted my eyes to the slaughter block and there on the concrete slab lay the brown form that had once been a cow. To my amazement it was almost twice the size of life. All the sad old starved contours had gone. It was a huge brown balloon and even the legs were puffy ugly appendages. The few men present were very busy. Two were engaged in pumping air with a bicycle pump into the dead thing, by means of a tube inserted under the hide. Two others were beating the poor blown-up beast in such a way that the air was being forced all round the carcass under the hide. When this macabre operation was over, it was possible, by making a long cut down the belly, to remove the hide, which peeled away just like the shedding of an old coat. On all sides squatted rows and rows of little boys, silent at last. I will not try to defend myself: like them I was glued there watching, half with horror, half with interest.

Then they slung the old flayed carcass to the overhead bar and the butchers of the village came for their quotas. The small boys drifted noisily back to the tomb and the episode was over.

Gradually the contents of the grave were transferred
to the Camp House and to other hands, where the pottery
was washed, marked, registered, mended if it were
broken, and eventually it all came to John in the drawing-
office. Here he makes a perfect drawing of the elevation
and section of each pot. It is from the vessels themselves
and from drawings such as these that the whole study of
pot-typology is made. Not only does John draw the pottery, but also all the 'finds' from the tombs and the Tell:
combs, rings, figurines, carved bone inlay, scarabs,
'cult objects' and so on.

The evening of the slaughter I tried to interest him in
the spate of miniature Early Bronze Age pots that would
presently be descending upon him. Incidentally and
unwisely, I related the sad saga of the morning's
butchery. Pots were forgotten and the sadness of the
remembered scene escaped him. The visual picture alone
impressed.

'Oh, but what colour,' was his comment. 'Just think of
it. That magnificent splash of crimson against the varying
greys of the mud houses.'

Poor John! I am afraid the stern discipline of black and white archaeological drawing was beginning to tell upon his Van Gogh soul. Every now and again he escaped and splashed bold colours on to paper: sometimes his inspiration came from the glowing peasant women at the stream or from the luscious green of the oasis.

Even our dear old off-whitewashed rooms were not immune when the colour mood came upon him. A perfectly harmless little passage was transformed into a gay Arab sitting-room. He ingeniously cut a stencil and daubed the most brilliant 'tiles' along the length of the two walls; red ink scarlet on one side, Reckitt's blue on the other. Reed mats were placed on the floors, and here, with legs outstretched in front of us, we leant back against the variegated walls and sipped the pre-dinner alcohol. Some of the more sober among us protested a little at the garishness of the colour scheme, but the protest was treated with proper contempt. John 'felt' red ink and Reckitt's blue, and that was how it was going to be. Night after night we squashed into our narrow Arab sitting-room, and quite soon we hardly noticed that the 'tiles' were there: they became part of our ramshackle home.

The sitting-room which, as I have said, was really a passage, led to a small balcony overlooking the pool. When the evenings became warmer it was enchanting to sit on this balcony and watch the women drawing water, the innumerable children arguing, and the coming and going of men and beasts. And behind them the Tell towers up. The highest point on the mound now is of the Early Bronze Age – in most areas the dwellings of later peoples have been eroded or quarried away.

Stand on this highest point and look out over the Jordan Valley. The scene has not changed much in the centuries. Our ancient Jerichoan will have looked beyond the green of his oasis to the white mud labyrinth of the Jordan, and to the Dead Sea. On all sides, but for his cultivation, he would see desert slopes hemmed in with mountains. Straight across the Valley, if his eyes were keen, he would recognize a town – Tell Iktanu – which

now is but a mound like his own. Only to the north-west
has the scene really changed. Clustered at the far end of
his town he would be puzzled by the myriad mud houses,
very similar to those in the town behind him. Four thousand years separate him from the Refugee Village of
today.

All round him the great walls of his town defended the
citadel: and they were indeed strong defences. From a
solid mud-brick wall resting on stone foundations, the
slope of the Tell descended sharply for thirty-three feet to
a double ditch some twenty-six feet below. Behind these
ramparts the townsmen felt secure from sudden attack.
But earth tremors in the Valley had brought their walls
tumbling, and in the end they appear to have been
overcome by fire. The evidence left in the earth is clear.
On either side of the strongly built penultimate wall a
layer of ash had accumulated. Presumably the attackers
had thrown fire brands on to the reed-thatched roofs of
the houses, which may even have been built on the line
of the wall itself. With the roofs in flames, the woodwork
of the doors and shutters would soon have caught, and
the collapsing houses would have deposited the burnt
layer that we see today. Outside the wall the attackers
may even have kept fires going to ward off the defence.
We do not really know how these mud cities were
burnt; but we have the evidence of scorched and
broken mud bricks, of ash, and of destruction.

The last of the Early Bronze Age people rallied themselves after this attack. They set to work to build their
last wall. It was a hastily constructed affair; they could
not even stop to bank up the foundations with earth, but
built the mud superstructure on the loosely thrown heaps
of stone. There was no time to make new mud bricks:
old ones, scorched and broken, sufficed for the last wall.
But all that feverish effort appears to have been of no
avail: once more they were attacked and this time they
were overwhelmed again by fire. Against the outer face
of the defences we have found a deep deposit of fine ash.
It lies against the stone foundations and for a depth of
almost three feet against the wall. The ash is fine and

beautiful to look at; there are bands of salmon pink and
pearly grey. But to the inhabitants it had meant destruction. The flames had licked through the open spaces
between the stones, drawn inwards by the draught.
More and more thornbush and reed must have been
thrown on to the fire and the ash piled up until the wall
was burnt to its very core. At what stage our townsmen
fled we do not know, but after the destruction of this wall
there is not a trace of them to be found upon the Tell.

We dig, record and photograph; but sometimes I
think what heartless people we are as we burrow down
and unravel the history of this mound. 'How interesting,'
we say: 'here is magnificent evidence for the end of the
Early Bronze Age.' But to our ancient Jerichoans it was a
real and living nightmare: it was indeed the end for them.

Other towns in Palestine were being similarly attacked.
If not fire, then fear must have driven the inhabitants
from their citadels. Slowly, through the length and
breadth of the countryside, the great old ways were
forgotten as a new and virile people rampaged through
the land.

CHAPTER SIX

Wandering Tribes

(2100-1900 B.C.)

THREE thousand years or more had passed since our first town-dwellers had raised their walls on the natural rock near the Spring. Jericho was, by now, a veteran town.

It was about the year 2100 B.C. that the Early Bronze Age folk were defeated and faded into oblivion. The new-comers were a semi-nomadic people who were invading Palestine and destroying the established towns. It is thought that they may have been Amorites, the people of the land or mountains of Martu (Syria). The Sumerians in the valleys of the Tigris and Euphrates called them the people of the West and considered them barbarians. There is extant a bitter Sumerian text referring to the Amorite – 'The weapon is his companion, he digs the Kamunu by the side of the mountain, and he knows no submission. He eats uncooked meat and he has no house in his lifetime.' This is a complaint from one who had clearly suffered from the incursions of these marauders; and it is quite reasonable to suppose that they were the conquerors of Jericho also, and of many of the other Palestinian towns.

The archaeological evidence consistently reveals a period of destruction. Many of the great walled citadels of Palestine cease to exist as prosperous towns and the land is given over to nomadic and semi-nomadic tribes-men who introduce new pottery forms, a new style of architecture and a new method of burying the dead. In no way can this period be called an advance in man's endeavour. These semi-nomadic invaders contributed nothing. In later years the Amorites became quite respectable and even produced in the eighteenth century

B.C. one of the world's greatest law-givers – Hammurabi, King of Babylon. But we encounter them at Jericho in their early, crude and rampaging days. Even so, I am always rather grateful to these Amorites for emerging as personalities at all from the amorphous blurr of 'ite-ish peoples who litter the pages of history for the next few centuries. These are Elamites, Kassites, Jebusites, Hivites, and so on, all equally confusing – but now we can look an Amorite in the eye and know that it was he, most probably, who built the bonfires round Jericho and squatted by the embers.

The defensive ditches of the Early Bronze Age surrounding the town filled up in time with débris washed down from the mound by the winter rains. You can see the ditches now in the side of the cutting silted up with mud, buried and forgotten.

The newcomers did not bother about a protecting wall; after all, they were the strong marauders – of whom should they be afraid? They appear to have camped about the Tell and the surrounding countryside, most probably in tents. Often in our search for tombs our trial-pits have revealed the fragmentary remains of a camping site consisting of blackened earth and potsherds. Later, on the Tell, they built themselves small houses, and we have traced the lines of walls built only to the thickness of a single brick.

At one place upon the mound we unearthed a sad relic from their times. It consisted of a small hole cut beneath the foundations of a wall, and round the hole stones had been carefully placed. Among the encircling boulders was a small bundle of human bones, that had once been a baby's, but were not lying in a natural position. Each tiny bone was separate in the jumble as though the little creature had possibly been boiled and gathered up into a containing cloth and laid among the stones. Was this, in fact, some sacrificial offering in the foundations of a ceremonial building? How was it that a dismembered baby found itself so carefully placed in this little monument?

Apart from the rudimentary houses and this mysterious

pit very little of the vigour and the energy of these tribesmen was wasted upon architecture, nor were they artists.
Theirs must have been a carefree unencumbered existence, eked out among their flocks and herds. Provision
for the dead appears to have been their major interest.
Each member of that wild community was provided with
a separate grave. Very occasionally we have found two
burials in one tomb, but usually a single burial was
placed in each.

At the moment we have found four types of tomb belonging to this phase, and it is thought that the dissimil-
arity is due to local differences in tribal customs rather
than to a chronological sequence of different invaders.

So we must imagine the Tell and the countryside
round about inhabited by various tribes of Amoritic
stock. They may even have clustered their tents together
in tribal batches, much as the Bedu Arabs do today, each
group adhering to its own accepted traditions.

And now you must come back with me to Area A,
because it was here amid the flies and smells and small
boys that a great number of the type we call the 'Dagger
tombs' were found. These were neat, nice little tombs
cut into the soft limestone, and their name is derived
from the fact that the dead man is generally accompanied
by a copper dagger about five inches long. Usually there
is a well-shaped circular shaft, about three feet in diameter, which descends for anything between three feet
to six feet. On the floor of the shaft there is an opening
into a small tomb-chamber about three feet by four
by three, at a lower level and to one side – the roof of the
chamber is only a little higher than the floor of the shaft.
The doorway in ancient times after the burial was
blocked by a large stone from the wadi and the shaft was
filled with earth. The dead man had been placed in a
crouched position with his knees drawn up and his arms
folded on to his chest. Near him his friends had put his
dagger. Sometimes, instead of the dagger, we found a
bronze pin and beads, and as far as we could determine
from the skeletal remains it had been the men who had
been buried with the daggers and the women with the

pins and beads (although this was not an invariable rule). As I squashed into these small tomb-chambers with my dead companions I often used to think how peaceful and

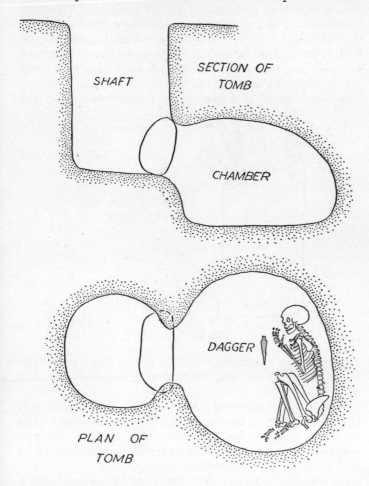

at rest the dead appeared. My feelings may be accentuated on these occasions by the utter physical discomfort in which I usually find myself at the time; crouched half in and half out of the tomb with a drawing board that, to

hand, obliterates all view, or else is inconveniently beyond reach in the shaft outside. Dust and dirt blow gently
but steadily into the shaft, and small boys cluster round
and watch the proceedings with fascination, knocking
in more dust and blocking out more light. We had heard
that the boys were a trial when I was setting out for the
first time to Jericho and at parting my small daughter
gave me her two water pistols with assurances that these
would keep the boys at bay. She put them in my writing
case, and often as I saw them I wondered what the

repercussions among the urchins of the Refugee Village
would be if I retaliated one day with a well-aimed blast
of water.

We found numbers of these Dagger tombs, and in each
the same story or nearly so; the daggers differed a little
in shape and size and to those who are studying the
weapons of this period our contributions from Jericho
add material for comparison.

It seemed to be my fate always to be jammed into a
Dagger tomb when the storks fly up the Jordan Valley.
Theirs is an annual migration from the south to the
gentler spring of more northern countries. Each year
about the middle of March we await their flight. I had

heard so much concerning this migration: how for half
an hour the Valley from horizon to horizon is speckled
with the great slow-flying birds. It must be a wonderful
sight to see thousands of them pushing northward with
head and neck thrust forward and the huge back and
white wings nonchalantly sweeping the air. I have been
curled like a hibernating mole in some Dagger tomb, and
I have been told when I have emerged how majestically
they flew.

'But you must call me,' I have reiterated time and
time again.

'Yes, Sitt, but we were so busy watching. We could not
remember where you were.' And so I have missed them,
or, at best, seen groups of stragglers. I blame my Dagger
tribesmen for this loss.

As the Refugee Village turned from an encampment
into a town of permanent mud-brick houses, it became
more and more difficult to find ground in which to search
for tombs. We now knew that the cemetery area must
stretch for a considerable distance under the village. By
degrees we had searched the open spaces and at last only
the streets had been left to us. The Refugees and the
Camp authorities had been most long-suffering. As we
dug along the lines of the roads, the enormous rumbling
water lorries and supply vans had continually to circum-
vent our excavation dumps. And then a whisper went
round the village that we were still eager for more
tombs, and some genius thought of probing in his own
back yard. Yes, he had found a tomb. Excited faces kept
reporting to Diana: 'Come, there is a tomb in my
house.'

The whole village was on to it – our tombs became
scattered about amongst the houses. What method we
had in digging for our graves vanished, and our daily
rounds became hot and dusty route marches from
'suburb' to 'suburb'.

Our welcome in each home is touching. Tea is brewed
the moment we step through the area gateway, and the
women of the household stare at us with eyes of wonder
as though we are creatures from another planet. I

suppose our trousers and bare arms, and our authority
over their men folk place us in a category of women un-
dreamed of in their minds. Some of them are very beautiful, with dark eyes and long lashes, and pleasing olive
skins. On their heads they wear little caps stitched all
over with beads and coins, and over and above this
flows a veil like a cloak, which can be used to conceal the
beauty of their embroidered dresses, their jewellery and
their faces when a man should pass. Their jewels are
silver trinkets and gaudy beads, and hidden amongst the
finery that hangs about their necks I often noticed a
necklet that puzzled me. One day I could restrain my
curiosity no longer and I asked a very friendly girl of
what the ornament consisted. She took the string from
her neck and handed it to me, and by her actions she

indicated that I was to smell it. The necklace was of
cloves strung head to tail on two threads, and after every
eighth clove she had placed blue beads – and then more
cloves. As decoration it was most effective, and at the
same time it provided the fragrant perfume that evidently the simplest woman desires to have. Their feet are
bare, and the palms of their hands are often stained with
henna. By degrees we became accepted in the homes of
the village people, and welcoming faces were turned to
us as we invaded the privacy of their lowly houses.

Within the walls of a small courtyard we found a
grave belonging to another tribal group. The shaft,
instead of being circular and typical of the Dagger type,
was square – and had been hewn square with deliberation right down to the floor. For the rest, the tomb-
chamber and the single burial with bronze dagger was
much the same. We have only found three or four of this
type: the Great Sitt has called them the 'Ajjul' type tombs,
because square-shafted Dagger tombs such as these have
been found in some numbers at the site of Tell el-Ajjul,

farther to the south on the coastal strip of Palestine. In one of these tombs we found, besides the dagger, a bronze spearhead similar to those found also at Ajjul.

In this group we came upon the Sultan – or so we called him. He must have been an important warrior. His grave was larger than is usual, and he did not lie crouched in humble sleep but full length across his tomb. Boldly they had placed him, and two daggers were by his hand. On his skull, which in death had rolled a little backwards, he wore a bronze fillet; by his shoulder

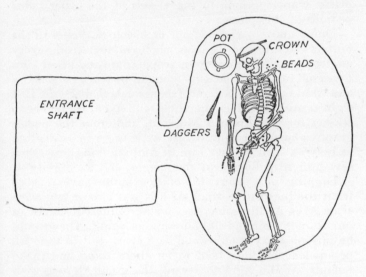

had been placed a decorated pot; small bronze studs lay embedded in the dust about his daggers and near his chest. There were fragments of wood and leather and even morsels of his desiccated flesh had dropped to the floor beneath his thighs. He was our treasure for some time. I will tell you later how it is that flesh and wood and leather have here survived the centuries, but for the moment we will think of him just as we found him.

He was old – there was hardly a tooth in his head – and he was tall with great long bones. Poor old fellow – I am afraid he must have suffered with arthritis, because the articulating surfaces of his joints were roughened and there was a horrid little bony growth near his elbow. But crotchety as he must have been, his followers respected him, and had laid him out with dignity in full regalia. More than likely the bronze studs were the vestiges of scabbards and strapping, and carnelian beads lay across his throat.

Pottery is very rare in these 'Ajjul' tombs and never before has such a pot as his been found, but in type it was of the period, with the distinctive flat base and hard gritty ware common to the vessels of the other tribal peoples of this phase.

Diana and I performed our archaeological rites in the Sultan's tomb and he was photographed from every angle: then the conservation people came and lifted him. I was sad to see him go. One moment he was a personality and the next but a box of bones labelled Tomb L 2 right femur, left tibia, mandible, and so on. He had been chosen for the Amman Museum, and from the photographs and my scale drawings he is to be reconstructed as he was. You will see him in Amman lying just as we saw him with his crown and dagger, and his dignity.

Digging in the courtyards of these houses gave us peace from the inquisitive small boys. It was almost sanctuary after Area A. But sometimes we encountered sadness in our rounds – a blind child or an idiot youth. They would be pushed away from us and kept apart. But in time we persuaded the household to let them come and make friends. At the Ajjul courtyard, the small Ahmed, with not an eyeball in his head, soon learnt to fossick his way round the dump, and would stand waiting hopefully for his 'Good morning. It is a pleasing day' and 'How are you?' To all of which he would respond, 'I am very well, praise be to Allah.' If only he could be taught a craft, the burden of his days would be lighter; but as things stand now, he will spend his time a groping body in this Refugee Village.

When we were digging in the open spaces and in the roads, the blind were quite a problem to us because of the danger of our open shafts. But fortunately they soon learnt that the encircling dump must on no account be crossed.

Another tragic fellow is the deaf, dumb and blind man who sits outside his house all day by the corner of the street where we found the 'Ajjul' tomb. I often wondered what he was thinking about. He can have no words because no one has taught him. Can one think without words? Or does he merely sense heat, cold, hunger, fatigue and sometimes, I hope, well-being. I

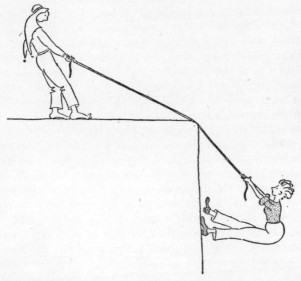

have known the little boys to throw pebbles at him too, and he makes strange noises. He will follow the shade round his house; but for the rest there is nothing. I think he must be about forty, and sometimes I have wished that Allah would call him to his reward.

Life in this Refugee Village cannot be greatly different from the life our tribesmen led about the Tell, nearly four thousand years ago.

The third and fourth types of tomb of this period consist of great deep shafts at the bottom of which spacious tomb-chambers have been cut. We found these big tombs scattered consistently all over the area, both in the open spaces and in the courtyards. Sometimes the shaft was as much as fifteen feet deep, and since the graves had become scattered after the private-house era began, it was an irksome business always to send for the ladder in order to descend into the chamber for planning and excavation. So, *faute de mieux*, we had to scale the sides. One press-ganged the nearest basket-boy with his rope and stationed him at the top with strict injunctions to lean back hard and take the weight. At the beginning I clung far too near the wall as I slithered down; but in time one develops a technique in everything, and eventually I attained a suitable nonchalance – behind well out, legs at right angles to the shaft, and a pretty action as I walked up and down the vertical walls. I felt this was almost a parlour trick, and I am afraid I may have swanked a little as I nipped in and out of these deep pits. But Nemesis was soon to follow. Having dismissed my anchor I was at the mercy of time and the verbal arrangements I had made. Perhaps the anchor had been told to return in half an hour, and perhaps, as happened on one frustrating occasion, I found myself down the wrong tomb. Bellowing is useless. Hardly a sound seems to make its way up the deep shaft, and if it does it will not turn at right angles at the top and permeate the countryside, but continues upward to be lost in the blue. I felt like an earwig in a bath, and even made pathetic attempts to scale the sides unaided, just as earwigs do. Poor earwigs, I have a fellow feeling for them. It was a long and useless half-hour which I spent, lying on my back inside the tomb surrounded by the scattered remnants of an Amoritic warrior.

There is a problem about the burial-customs of this particular tribal group. Having dug an enormous burial chamber ten feet high, and twelve by six feet on plan, our ancient people proceeded to inter one solitary fellow. Actually we have found three femurs in one tomb, so I must correct that statement – they proceeded to inter possibly one-and-a-bit fellows. But it is the method that is puzzling. Sometimes the spine lies in articulation, with

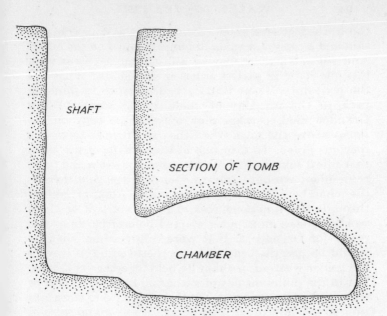

SHAFT

SECTION OF TOMB

CHAMBER

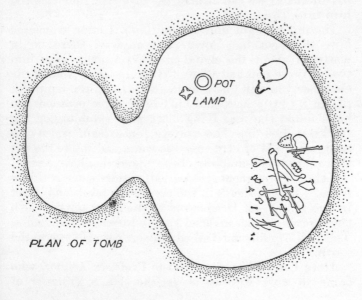

POT

LAMP

PLAN OF TOMB

the limbs scattered about. Sometimes the skull is to one side and a conglomeration of bones is found on the other. And yet again there may be a disarticulated array with just one hand in perfect order in their midst. What was the procedure? There is macabre fascination in thinking back to the actuality of these burial scenes. When Grandpa died, perhaps they exposed the body on the slopes above the town while they set to work to dig his spacious grave. To clear one of these shafts of the earth that fills it takes two of our team about a week; and then, remember, we have only to open the door and there is the chamber. Theirs was the initial work of cutting through the limestone rock. Let us say two or three weeks at least must have elapsed before the tomb was ready for Grandpapa. If it were summertime, then he would be just the bone melange that we find; if it were the colder weather, perhaps he held together yet a little, but in the pulley-hauley of gathering him up, an arm or leg may have come away. Yet they managed to wrap him up and get him to his final home. There are no signs of cut marks so we can dismiss the idea that they chopped him into 'ritual' bits.

Having brought him to the tomb, I often wondered how they got him down. But anyway, there he is, scattered about the chamber. They usually gave him two or three pots and a lamp. High up on the wall of the chamber you will find a niche. Sometimes the lamp still sits in its little hole, and on two or three occasions we have found the wick lying black and crumbling on the smoke-stained lip. The pottery, once seen, is easy to recognize: it is of hard metallic ware, and inside the pot there is always a dimpling of the fingers that have pressed the clay. Throughout this period, pottery such as this is found – broken sherds in the occupation levels and intact in the tombs – at Jericho and at the other towns which these semi-nomads invaded and destroyed: towns such as Tell Beit Mirsim and Tell ed Duweir near Hebron to the south.

Here I must introduce you to Professor Zeuner, who came to work with us at Jericho. He is Professor of

Environmental Archaeology in the University of London; which means that he studies the living-conditions of early man: his surroundings, the climate, the animals and plants he had to cope with and, last but not least, the raw materials that he won from his environment. In addition, the Professor is much concerned with geo-chronology, which is a long way of saying the art of dating things in years where the historical calendar no longer helps us. Wherever he appears he plays the detective, indulging in sinister scientific tricks to find out what happened, and when.

In particular he came to study the animal bones found on the Tell and in the tombs, and to unravel the mystery of the preservation in these tombs of such fragile materials as reeds, wood and even flesh. I will tell you of his labours in the next chapter, but for the moment he comes into our story and into one of the deep-shafted tombs with a new and knowing eye. He spotted at once the termite (white ant) galleries and the ant-lions' craters, and to him these tiny vestiges told their story. With these few clues and with samples of earth that he took from the floor of the tomb, he was able to tell us certain facts about the tomb and method of burial. After the gravel had been dug, the door remained open long enough for wind-blown dust to settle on the floor. His cutting through the thin accumulation on the floor showed that on two or three occasions the dust had been swept to one side of the chamber. In this slight mounding of the dust were two ant-lion larva funnels. At the bottom of each of these tiny craters ant-lion larvae had waited hopefully for their prey. Poor silly ants had tumbled down the shaft of the tomb and in their pathetic wanderings had slithered into the traps, only to be snatched by the waiting jaws of the concealed larvae, who sucked them dry and flicked their useless skins out of the funnels. And there, to be found by the Professor, were the discarded and desiccated remains of ancient ants around the ensnaring little craters.

Some time, therefore, must have passed between the digging of the tomb and the sealing of the door, and sun-light will have blazed into the shaft and been reflected into the chamber, because ant-lions are sun-worshippers and are not found in closed and hidden caverns. I suggest that there may have been a city grave-digger who dug tombs by the dozen, and who occasionally did the rounds and swept them clean, until such time as they were needed. Then a day would come, and a grave be bought for a burial. The body – or the bundle of bones – was wrapped up. Not a vestige of the wrapping remains, but from the presence of the termite galleries we can deduce that this was so. The bundle of bones was brought to the tomb. The door was sealed, the shaft filled. It was the end.

But we, who come thousands of years later, know that this was not quite the end. Down through the crevasses in the limestone, busy little termites always on the prowl for food scented the vegetable matter that encased the body. Their habit is to build mud-tunnels or galleries, and these galleries can be seen leading from the cracks down the wall of the chamber right up to the very bundle of bones. Termites will not touch flesh, so we can surmise that they came possibly for a reed mat in which the corpse had been wrapped and in which it had been transported to the tomb. If it were a mat, then the ends of the parcel would have been open; and as it was thrown into the chamber, the skull could easily have rolled out and come to rest at a distance from the main group, which is how we so often found it. Limbs, or a vertebra or two, could easily have slipped out. Then stillness but for the microscopic activities of the termites. Perhaps, as happened in some of the tombs, an earth tremor brought the lamp crashing from its niche in the wall, and a few limestone blocks may have been dislodged from the ceiling. Thereafter, the long spell of nothingness until we came.

The fourth and last type of tribal tomb was almost the same except that the shafts were not so deep and the tomb chambers more carelessly cut. In each of these poorer graves we found the same scattered bones, but there were no pottery gifts at all, only an occasional bronze stud. A mean tribe.

But all these Amoritic tombs began to repeat themselves with an element of monotony. On occasions our attention might pardonably wander to the more modern interests of the area in which we found ourselves. This lay near the simple mud mosque in the Village, and at noon and at three o'clock the picturesque old Muezzin would make his way on to the roof and chant the Islamic call to prayer. His reedy voice would waver out over our heads and momentarily there would be silence in the school tents near us. In these tents the little boys of the Village sit for hours and hours, learning. We soon got to know which lessons were in progress by the sound or lack of sound from the tents. Complete silence meant arithmetic, occasional mumblings indicated that an English lesson was in progress, rhythmic sing-song chanting was the Koran, and uproar the period for patriotic uplift.

We thoroughly appreciated school days. The curious young were incarcerated in tents (now they are in magnificent school buildings) far from our excavations. Friday, their holy day, is, as I have said, a nightmare. The children are at large and we are the focus for their evergreen curiosity and their pranks. On school days patient bus-loads of teachers are driven up, each teacher trying to hold his own in face of daunting odds. On Fridays, *we* bear the brunt. Each school day when the battle is over the young emerge. There are hundreds of little boys with shaven colourful heads many of them dabbed here and there with gentian violet, the disinfectant of the East. They wear shorts and shirts, and nearly all carry small wooden boxes containing their exercise books. Some of them take it all very seriously: isosceles triangles are drawn out in the dust and earnest post-mortems ensue. Sometimes one of us is caught in an expansive mood and advice is sought, given and received. I remember how on one occasion I was captured by an advanced scholar who was in search of ideas for an essay. He wanted his essay to be about a river. As he said 'river', glimmerings of that tiresome poem flickered in my memory: 'Something, something, coot and hern' and

D

'something down the valley'. You know the thing. Between us we elaborated the theme. We grew from a babbling brook into a river nearly approaching the Rhine, and all the time he kept repeating 'and men may come and men may go, but I go on for ever'. He liked that. It was to be his dénouement, and he wrote it down verbatim. Later I wondered what his tired Egyptian master of English must have made of it. In fact, I often wondered whether all this teaching was worth while. Would it not be better to use the moneys, given by the world to these sad people, to reclaim the desert by irrigation and to resettle them as peasant farmers? Where? Of course that is the problem. But this smattering of Western knowledge will get them nowhere, and any sort of job is almost impossible to come by.

At the same time the little girls emerge in droves from the school houses with the unimaginative hand of the 'progressive' West upon them too. They wear scanty black cotton uniforms with white plastic collars, the edges of which have been stencil-cut to look like lace. Plastic strings tie this monstrosity at the neck. It is connected to no part of the dress and swivels at will. One moment it is the right way on and the next it is back to front. A masterpiece of invention! Who *is* it who thinks of a thing like this? In its way, of course, it is genius. The plastic will never wear out, never get dirty.

Our last excavation of an Amoritic tomb in this school area has left us with a mystery. Digging close to a mud house our workmen located a shaft, and joyfully reported a tomb. We instructed them to dig outwards until they hit the wall of the shaft and to clear the surface earth away until the entire rim was exposed. It was possible to see as they shovelled away the earth that we were on to the circular entrance of one of the deep tribal tombs. But it was a pit such as we had never seen before. The curve of the walls was stretching out into a circumference much larger than any we had previously had, and to our consternation we realized that the neighbouring mud house was built over a segment of the shaft. It was so huge and so spectacular an entrance that the Great Sitt felt it was worth the gamble to clear the huge pit to the bottom in the hope that the doorway would prove to be in the three-quarters of the shaft that we would be able to expose. A whole slice of filling was left uncleared to bear the weight of the side of the house above. It was a very deep entrance pit: deeper than any we had had. On size alone we felt this must be a most important grave. Our hopes and fears were soon felt at the Camp House, and progress was reported at each meal. Would we, or would we not, strike the door in the three-quarters of the shaft that we were able to dig? It was a three-to-one possibility. But there was no door. It lay tucked away, buried, in the segment of filling that we had to leave to support the house. I suppose we all knew in our hearts that the fates would frown. Undercutting was unthinkable. The earth filling of the shaft was too loose to play about with, and any attempt at an undercut hole would have exposed the workmen to the risk of being buried in an avalanche from above and the collapse of the house above that.

The owners of the little house watched our deliberations with acute anxiety, as well they might, for the possibility of buying the house and destroying it was seriously discussed. The price we were told would be thirty pounds. A house for thirty pounds! But the owners besought the Great Sitt not to move them. This, and the fact that time was short and our funds were very low, saved them. It was sad for us to have to fill in the great shaft. What lay behind that metre of earth? Now, at this moment, he lies undisturbed in his huge tomb chamber – and we do not know whether he is a very special gentleman in full regalia or whether he is just another of the poor fellows scattered in pieces round about his pots.

All through this ancient tribal period Transjordan and Eastern Palestine were steadily becoming depopulated; the nomadic and semi-nomadic tribesmen had successfully reduced the countryside to a wilderness. But Palestine was on the Egyptian trade-route. Some attempt had to be made to keep the country open. No doubt the coastal strip was patrolled by force, because the archaeological evidence shows that Western Palestine soon recovered and became more settled, and Egyptian influence extended right through into Phoenicia and Syria. But it must have been anxious work, because the Egyptians resorted to little protective magics. They inscribed the names of rebels and potential rebels on pots and vases. When occasion demanded, they ceremonially broke the vases, for they believed that by so doing they were breaking the power of the enemy. Hoards of these broken inscribed pots have been discovered and are known as the Execration Texts. From a study of the Texts it is possible to infer the extent of Egyptian control. The boundary lay somewhere north of Damascus in central Syria. But the power of Egypt was weakening, and in time it fell to the northern peoples to infuse their genius into a new culture which gradually became established in Palestine.

CHAPTER SEVEN

The Shepherd Kings

(THE MIDDLE BRONZE AGE: 1900-1580 B.C.)

THE newcomers were from the north. Imperceptibly the semi-nomadic tribesmen on the Tell melted away, as yet we do not know how or why, and a new culture replaced the old. The tribal movements of the period are almost impossible to trace. But the fact remains that throughout the length and breadth of Palestine there was change. In time those who brought or adapted themselves to the new conditions became known as Canaanites.

At Jericho these Canaanites appear to have blotted out the former way of life completely. No trace of an intermingling is apparent in the occupation-levels that continued gradually to accumulate upon the Tell. And then, perhaps a century and a half later, they accepted and absorbed a warrior aristocracy known to history as the Hyksos or Shepherd Kings. These new overlords, also from the north, introduced chariotry and a new style of defensive rampart. What with the artistic achievement of the Canaanites and the drive and military wisdom of the Hyksos, these Middle Bronze Age people became a power in the land. Their towns grew and prospered. One by one great citadels sprang up on the decayed mounds of the earlier towns. The Hyksos rulers spread their dominion farther and farther to the south and eventually, in 1730 B.C., they conquered Egypt.

The new Hyksos wall at Jericho was a tremendous achievement. It encircled the Tell more or less on the line of the old Early Bronze defences. The slope of the mound was shorn away and layer after layer of marl and mud was plastered against it until a steep and regular slope had been formed all round the town.

At the top of this 'glacis' (as we call it, not very correctly) a stout mud-brick wall was erected. To an army attacking the town the slippery gradient of the glacis would present a formidable obstacle and effectively keep the attackers at some distance from the crowning walls. In our great cutting through the mound it is possible to see that three of these huge defences were successively constructed. The first was the strongest and it must have lasted for a considerable period. Here and there it was patched. It must have soared up from a stone retaining wall, but this was removed when the second rampart was constructed. This in turn was mutilated and buried when the third and last defensive girdle was built about the town. Here we have a strong stone wall, built upon the natural rock, and from the top of this they carried the slope or glacis upward to the city walls.

One day I was called upon to plan a skeleton which had been unearthed at the foot of this stone revetment. It was the skeleton of a woman. She had been buried outside the town at the base of the towering wall. Everything about her was dainty and she lay curled up in a neat position. It would not take me long, I knew, to make a scale drawing of anything so orderly. Elizabeth, the site supervisor, gave me the measurements and together we plotted the position of her spine. At her neck we stopped and looked at each other in amazement. She had had her head chopped off. The break in the sequence of the vertebrae was obvious: the skull and the few top joints were seriously out of position. Our sudden realization of how she had met her death rather horrified us. We had been drawing, a few minutes before, the sad remains of a dead woman, but now we were engaged in measuring the limbs of a victim of murder or execution. There was an eerie quality about her. Some of the other supervisors could not control their curiosity and came to see her. Poor little thing. One could not help but wonder why she had been killed. Had she been offered in sacrifice and buried at the foot of the great wall? Had she been executed for crime? Was this the price of adultery? Who knows?

We were able to trace these massive defences three-quarters of the way round the town. Although we have not ourselves found an entrance, it most probably consisted of a ramp winding its way up to a double or triple gateway which gave entrance to the town. Such, at least, was the entrance through a similar 'glacis' defence farther south at Tell Beit Mirsim.

They were not peaceful times, but within these strong walls the Middle Bronze Age people lived and prospered. Unfortunately most of their town does not now exist. Perched as it was high up upon the mound it has long since disappeared. Violent destruction and the weathering of the centuries have washed much of it to the foot of its own defences, but the little that remains gives us an indication of the whole. On the eastern side of the town we have unearthed a street, cobbled and sloping. Where the slope has become too steep we have found steps. It is a mean and narrow way, but beneath it runs a drain. Giving on to this little alley are two or three houses, small but well constructed, and in the ground-floor rooms big pottery jars are stacked round the walls. On two or three occasions the walls of these houses have collapsed from earthquake tremors or from fire. The fire preserved for us great quantities of corn, charred and blackened, but still lying in the bins. This grain was a pleasant and unexpected source of income to our Excavation Fund; an enterprising member of the team sold small quantities of it to guileless trippers who appeared only too eager to exchange good money for handfuls of curious and antique grain.

Although our tiny corner of the Middle Bronze Age town is not impressive, from other sites we can learn how the patricians lived. Their houses were large and spacious and were built round an inner court. From the excavations at Tell Beit Mirsim it has been deduced that the living-quarters were in an upper storey and that the ground-floor rooms were used for storage, or in some cases for stabling. Often a great contrast is found between the houses of the rich and those of the poor. After the fall of Egypt, when the Hyksos were supreme, there are indications of some luxury.

But once again the tombs tell us more than does the town. These people of the Middle Bronze Age were generous to their dead, and everywhere the tombs are richly filled.

They were in the same area to the north of the Tell where all our other graves were found. They were not particular, these Middle Bronze Age people, about the size or shape of the tomb; they were content with a shallower shaft and smaller chamber than those of their predecessors. It was easier still, so thought their grave-diggers, to find an earlier shaft and empty it. The earth filling was soft and necessitated far less work than a new cutting in the limestone rock. And so it is that we find many of these burials in the deep and spacious tombs of the Amoritic tribesmen.

In some cases they had nice feelings and left the original skeleton as they found him on the floor. They merely covered him with a layer of earth and forgot that he was there. Sometimes they threw him out, and their own burials lie packed upon the rock floor in his place, but on the whole they were kind, and having covered him, they later laid their dead on top.

Their methods were simple and present no problems. Each one of their dead was brought to the tomb and laid full length upon the floor. Round about the corpse the gifts were placed. Obviously he needed substantial provisions for his long journey into the unknown, so they gave him food and drink and pottery vessels. Sometimes they added his weapons and his jewellery. A small oil lamp may have been lighted. Then they left him and closed the doorway with its huge rock boulder. But these were family graves and in the natural course of events his solitude could not last for long. His wife was sick and dying on the Tell. Soon she was brought to join him in the tomb. They roughly pushed him back. He had had his turn at peace upon the floor and she was given the central position. His gifts too were pushed away and hers were placed carefully about her. There were vessels and food too, no doubt, but especially for her they brought the dainty things. She had loved the little wooden bowl carved like a pomegranate. This they put into a basket with her finely carved combs, her carnelian necklace and a faïence perfume bottle. There was the alabaster dish with its four ram's head handles and the amethyst scarab that she had treasured as an amulet. All these lovely things they arranged about her. But in time she too was pushed aside.

One after another the bodies displaced each other until the sides and back of the chamber were piled high with displaced skeletons. Here and there an attempt had been made to stack the grave-goods by the walls, but the skeletons were allowed to become a casual melange. Sometimes they cleared the centre of the chamber and erected a low mud-brick platform, on which they laid the body. At other times they placed it on a board, or a reed mat. We found the remains of many tables and some stools. The tables were of interest because they showed the sockets for *three* legs only – one in the middle at one end, and the other two at either side at the far end. I am told that three legs placed thus obviate all wobble on rough ground. Sometimes the table tops were re-used as trays by later comers, who placed upon them their gifts of food. There were joints of mutton, sheep's heads, dishes of roasted flesh and bowls of raisins. The water-pots were there for drink, and in each we found the little dipper jug that was used to take the water from the heavy parent jar. There were also other pots for liquid, with sealed mouths. They stood about three feet high and were monstrous vessels. One of these big pots had been cracked and patched in ancient times, and as I measured up its sides and drew it on my plan, I could not help but think: 'You wicked little family. You buried old uncle with a shabby patched pot when you put this into his grave.' But on the other hand, we also found real generosity. In the depths of a cluttered tomb we came upon five beautiful gold rings, three of them set with amethysts. It cannot have been easy to give those jewels away.

As I crouched in the tombs alone with my Middle Bronze Age companions, I could not help but moralize upon their uneven solicitude for their dead. At the moment of burial they gave so much, the body was

D*

placed with such great respect and thoughtful attendance within the chamber. Later the same relatives could shove the deceased's head into someone else's basket and his own food-plate into his ribs. Did they think he did not mind lying in a muddle? If so, why so much ceremonial to begin with?

Professor Mylonas, writing of Mycenaean communal graves, tentatively suggests that 'the spirit of the departed was sentient and was around the grave as long as the flesh was in existence; the corpse was treated with respect; it had to be provided with supplies; it had to be given favourite objects that in life belonged to it; it had to be kept in the grave by walled doors. The moment the body was dissolved and was transformed into a pile of bones it no longer had need of anything; there was no danger that its spirit would reappear; the spirit had descended into its final abode never to return; the bones could be swept aside or even thrown out'. This may have been the underlying thought in the minds of our people too.

The larger tombs contained fifty or sixty burials, and the skeletons were of all ages. Not all the graves we found were completely full, and there were six that were particularly interesting because they contained a few undisturbed burials.

These tombs were, all except one, re-used from the earlier period; but they had been prepared suitably by our Middle Bronze Age folk, who had either removed the earlier skeleton and stacked his pottery in the shaft, or had covered him with earth and thus made a new surface. Into these six prepared graves a number of dead had been placed at the same time. In one of the chambers there were only four skeletons, and in the others as many as seven or nine. Two were privileged and lay on low mud platforms. In all cases the skeletons were outstretched one beside the other. There were no signs of violence upon the bones, so perhaps they were the victims of an epidemic; but whatever the disaster, they were gathered up and buried with generous solemnity. Their grave-goods lay about them in the positions in which they had

been placed so long ago. No hurly-burly of subsequent
burials had broken or disturbed the offerings.

And so in these tombs we are given as complete a
picture as is possible of the vessels, furniture and belong-
ings of the Middle Bronze Age people. Even fragments of
their textiles have survived, and in the baskets sometimes we find ropy stuffs that we think could be the
material of wigs. The women may have coiled their
black hair round their heads or let it fall in one rich plait
down their backs, augmented with this fabric. Such is the
feminine way, and so we see the Arab women of today

with their hair entwined with artificial tresses. Perhaps
the most dainty of all the treasures that have survived to
us are the small wooden boxes inlaid with carved bone.
This had been engraved with geometric designs or
carved into individual flat pieces representing jaunty
little birds and then set into the wooden sides of the
boxes. Alas, all the wood has shrunk about twenty per
cent, so that the bone-inlaid pieces have been squeezed
out, and now they merely lie in the order in which they
had been originally placed.

One little box particularly attracted admiration from
us all. It could boast of no bone inlay, but claimed attention because of its perfection and simplicity. It was a
little bigger than a match-box, the sides were fitted to
each other with delicate tenons, and the lid, which we
found closed, would slide open along two tiny ledges when

we pulled it by the small knob-handle attached at one end. Just basic box, but perfect, and an indication of the excellent joinery of which our Middle Bronze Age Jerichoans were capable.

In the roadway by the Mosque we found a unique tomb belonging to this group. The water lorries of the village good-naturedly took other tracks to avoid us. The urchins enjoyed our labours as, slowly, our pair of workmen cleared the shaft of an earlier tribal tomb. It was time for the door slab to be hauled back and we were all expectant. What lay behind that sealing boulder? So often before had our hopes been dashed that we approached the task with little more than routine expectation. The small stone packing round the door was removed, the stone slab itself was heaved aside and there before us was the tomb-chamber. The roof had not fallen – it was perfect. From one quick glance it was possible to

see that it was a Middle Bronze Age tomb; there were the water pots we knew so well. But this time it was different. Alone he lay outstretched on the floor – our warrior. All the other tombs of this period had contained multiple burials. Here, at last, we had found an aristocrat worthy of solitude.

He had been placed directly upon the floor to the left side of the tomb, which was roughly oblong. His head was nearest the door. The right arm lay full length beside him and his left arm had been placed across the body. One by one the bones of his disintegrating left hand had fallen into the basin of his hips. Most of his offerings had been placed at the far end of the tomb beyond his feet, but to right and left of him lay his weapons and accoutrement. Two bronze daggers with alabaster knob-handles and two axes were to the right side of the tomb, and beyond his body, against the wall, we found another axe and his beautiful bronze belt. This was about three inches

deep and twenty-seven inches round and was embossed
with a design of concentric circles. Although bronze belts
have been found elsewhere, our decorated one is unique.
Among the gifts at the back of the chamber were beads
and food and pottery vessels. As his friends left him, having placed their offerings, they put one last pot in the
doorway before they closed it, as they thought, for ever.
It was the most beautiful of all, with a pointed base and
open mouth, and on it the potter had moulded a ram's
head with horns sweeping backwards towards the rim.

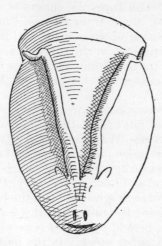

We had not had a pot like this before. In fact our warrior
was our pride for quite a time. Distinguished visitors
were encouraged to go down the shaft and crawl through
the particularly small doorway and gape at him. Poor
warrior! I hated seeing smart tweeded behinds come
shuffling backwards through the doorway into the shaft
after an invasion of his solitude.

Although the Middle Bronze Age tombs everywhere
are richly filled, ours at Jericho are richer still because in
them we find the furnishings which elsewhere have
vanished; the wooden objects, mats, baskets and foodstuffs. In them we often find the skeletons surrounded
with fragments of brownish matter that we have learnt

to recognize as partially disintegrated human flesh. Many a time inside a skull we have been able to see the dried-up brain.

It was a tremendous problem why these ephemeral things should have been preserved here and not elsewhere for more than three thousand five hundred years. In the normal course of events all organic matter rots away: busy little bacteria see to that. Sometimes in conditions of constant dryness or of constant dampness the microscopic organisms of decay are thwarted, and so we have the wonderful funerary objects of Egypt and the waterlogged bog 'finds' from Europe. But at Jericho we can disclaim neither of these extremes. It is a climate of dry and scorching heat in the summer and usually there are excellent rains for a month or two each winter. What then was the answer to this problem? Why is Jericho unique?

At this stage we appealed to another science to help us, and at the Great Sitt's invitation Professor Zeuner came to inspect our tombs. We showed him all our discoveries, from the dainty baskets to the dried-up brains. He spent hours down certain tombs taking samples of earth and rock for chemical and microscopic study. We even caught him sniffing broken fragments from the limestone walls. We all began doing it. Quite true, it was smelly. We had not noticed this before, because it is necessary to break a fresh piece and put it quickly to the nose to obtain the best results.

Every tiny thing seemed to be a clue and a pointer to him. He went for long excursions down the Valley and was gone for days. And then, at last, the morning came when he propounded his theory.

He believes that the tomb-chambers became filled with gases and that all the bacterial agents of decay themselves perished before their deadly work was done. It is quite possible, he told us, for subterranean gases to seep through the rock because here at Jericho we are situated on the western line of the Rift Fault. Jericho is built over one of the two cracks along which the Valley of the Jordan and the Dead Sea has been subsiding, between the mountains of Judah in the west and those of Moab in the east. This sinking of a narrow strip of the earth's crust has been going on for the last million years or so and it is still continuing. No wonder there are earthquakes for the movement of these big cracks cannot but be jerky. No wonder also that where the fault is situated the rock is cracked and crushed.

He showed us a band of flint where it was exposed in one of the tomb-chambers. It was a band of splinter chips; the smooth solidity of homely old flint was not there at all.

'And the limestone too is cracked through and through,' he told us. With a slight movement he prodded the roof of the chamber in which we were crouching, and a sizeable piece toppled easily into his hand.

Diana and I raised our eyebrows. Surely he was showing more enthusiasm than was necessary in this demonstration of how easily we could be either gassed or brained? What witless folk we were; this was nothing but an excellent geological demonstration of the possibilities of gas seeping through the earth's crust in this, the 'fault zone'.

Were we convinced, or would we like him to knock off another block of roof? We assured him that we were absolutely convinced that the limestone was thoroughly disturbed.

'Well, then, as a beginning,' he announced, 'we will carry out the schoolboy test for carbon dioxide.' He commanded us to find a new tomb immediately and to stop excavation the moment we located the door. It was to be left unopened.

Two of our workmen were far enough down a shaft for us to expect the door slab to show at any moment. We told them to continue down to the door and then to stop, and on no account were they to knock any of the earth packing away from the top of the slab. We explained that it was most important as we were going to carry out an experiment. 'Yes, Sitt, yes, yes.' They understood completely. But one or other of us should have stood above them to make assurance doubly sure. Those innocent villains came to the door slab and removed the packing

above enough to enable them to have a quick glance into
the chamber. It was a good tomb. The roof had not fallen.
They were happy that our experiment would be carried
out in a worthy chamber. Carefully they replaced the
packing; evidently we had wanted it like that, and they
emerged from the shaft. But innocent villains do not
stand a chance. Their clumsily replaced packing told a
guilty tale. Diana taxed them with their duplicity and
down they toppled.

'We were only seeing if it was a good tomb for the
experiment,' they expostulated.

But they could not save themselves and had to bear
the blast that followed instantly upon their admission.
We too, had learnt our lesson, and we sat like patient
vultures on the edge of another shaft and watched the
energetic shoulders of the men as they heaved the earth
away.

In the meantime, Professor Zeuner went off to the
Hospital and the Government Laboratories at Jerusalem
and persuaded the authorities to lend him pumps, tubes
and retorts, and the all-important bottle of lime water.
If carbon dioxide passes through lime water, it will turn
milky.

In due course we were able to rig up our apparatus
above ground. We were to have two comparative tests:
one of the surface atmosphere, and one of the air in the
tomb-chamber.

You must imagine us with yards of rubber tubing
connected to a small bottle of lime water, which in turn
was attached to a suction pump by still more tubing.
Neither Diana nor I knew much about chemistry, so this
was a profound moment. With the receiving tube held
boldly into the atmosphere of the Jordan Valley, Professor
Zeuner gave solemn pulls on the suction pump. For five
minutes, with fruity gasps, the Jericho air passed through
the lime water. Our eyes were riveted to the bottle, and
nothing happened. We had been told to expect nothing,
but for five minutes we feared that the atmosphere of
the Valley might let us down. Then we clambered into
the shaft and one by one the packing stones of our new

door were taken away and we opened a very small hole above the great stone. Through this we pushed the tube, which by now we had tied on to a long bamboo cane so that we could get it well into the chamber. With a fresh bottle of lime water attached, we began to pump. For a whole minute the clear water defied our exertions. My faith in Professor Zeuner's diagnosis remained firm, but I must admit I was becoming anxious. And then slowly the crystal clearness of the liquid vanished, and by degrees it became whiter and more opaque until at last we held a little bottle that appeared to be full of watered milk.

The smug feeling of success was tremendous: we had proved that a certain quantity of at least one gas was entrapped within the chamber.

The following year Professor Zeuner came again to Jericho and he brought with him a wonderful equipment for extracting, measuring and isolating gases. He bade us take samples of air from each tomb as we opened it, and then again from selected spots in the chamber as soon as we could enter it. In the tomb one of us would slither the receiving nozzle on to the floor, the other would pump slowly in the shaft. We would then label our glass container 'Air from the floor of Tomb X', 'Air from the basket No. 1, Tomb X', 'Air from the plate of meat, No. 2, Tomb X' and so on. It was amusing to note our nonchalance with the glass containers when we knew they were empty. We picked them up and handled them freely without any feeling of restraint. But after our pumping operations, an earnestness overcame us and we handed the same seemingly empty glass container from one to the other with elaborate care. Visually nothing had changed – it looked still an empty receptacle, but we knew that now it was filled with air sucked from between the ribs of a Middle Bronze Age Jerichoan.

After each session we gave Professor Zeuner his bottles full of air. He worked for hours in what he called his laboratory. This consisted of an enormous box on the verandah of a small mud-brick cottage near the Camp House. In that box he had devised a machine, consisting of glass tubes and taps and mercury and bulbs. And here at this Machine – I will give it a capital M – the Professor was able to isolate various gases and to measure their proportions.

At the time of writing he can tell us that there is a fairly high proportion of methane gas and carbon dioxide. But neither of these, he tells us, would be sufficient to destroy the bacterial agents of decay. There are still other gases to be isolated and to be studied, and perhaps among these he will find the gas or gases responsible for the extraordinary preservation in our tombs. That it is a gas he feels certain, because the evidence within the tombs themselves points in that direction. Normal organic decay began and then for some reason was arrested. Even the termites, whose little mud-built galleries we can see leading from the crevices to the vegetable matter within the tombs, did not finish their job. Something as yet unknown to us deterred them. They began their feasts upon the wood and reeds and baskets, and then were overwhelmed. Indeed, some of the mud galleries of the later comers are incomplete. They withdrew or died before they even reached the goal.

It's tantalizing, but soon I feel we shall know the answer. We must keep Professor Zeuner chained to The Machine.

So there they are, our rare and rich tombs, giving us a remarkably complete picture of those far-off Middle Bronze Age Palestinians.

From the excavator's point of view, these graves were very difficult. There was nowhere to place a foot, and we had to work inwards slowly from the doorway, photographing and preserving, measuring, drawing and recording. I do not know whose task was the most tricky. Perhaps, in fact, it was the photographer's. This was Nancy, who was expected to take first-class studies of everything, stationed as she usually was between fragile baskets and jumbles of flesh and bones. One foot carelessly placed could obliterate for ever a carved wood pomegranate box or coil of wig-material. Photography at the best of times is a sport that calls for much patience and

evenness of temper. Anyone who can frolic about under
that black velvet shroud and emerge minutes later with
the same good humour is indeed a long-suffering character. But he, or she, who can import these instruments of
aggravation into a cluttered tomb and still remain at
peace with the world is a rare companion. Such a one is
Nancy.

Down she would come into the shaft, complete with
monstrous boxes, an unsympathetic photographic tripod
and the black velvet. We would see her disappear through
the small doorway, dragging one or other of her ungainly
pieces of equipment after her. We would switch on the
generator so that she could arrange yet another tripod,
the one carrying the electric light, to suit herself. We
could offer no help on these occasions because there is
rarely room for one plus photographic paraphernalia, let
alone two. She suffered alone. Flashlight photographs
can be taken, but they are not as good as the time-studies
because the shadows are too hard. A time-exposure with
artificial lighting reflected from the roof or the walls of
the chamber melts the shadows and a much better picture
is the result. Sometimes, if the natural illumination from
the doorway is good enough, it is possible for a fairly
lengthy time-exposure to do the work unaided; but, in
whatever way it is done, it is a long and cramping
business.

There are, of course, the lighter moments that relieve
the gloom. One afternoon Nancy was gingerly arranging
herself in an overloaded family tomb when she found
that the electric tripod was not sufficiently well placed.
Choosing a fresh foothold she leant forwards to adjust
the light, and slowly, to the left, a lower jaw closed upwards with a click to meet the upper teeth of a skull that
gazed at her with hollow eyes. She did not adjust the
light and unconsciously recoiled. The jaw dropped open
and the skull grinned back at her. We are not all so
scientifically minded that little things like this mean
nothing. Nancy is the first to admit that for the moment
she thought, 'My tombs days are over. This sort of thing
can't go on. Now I have seen one chattering skull, others

are sure to follow.' With rather a solemn 'by your leave'
to the skull in question, she resolutely stepped forward
once again and as she gripped the tripod the jaw snapped
upwards. It was an absurd relief when it had happened
again. What were the mechanics of that step? Bending
down, she examined the débris beneath her feet. Chance
had placed three long bones at random across the tomb:
her foot, pressing on the end of one had levered the
second, the second bone levered the third, which lifted
the jaw into position.

Working in these tombs we do become almost uncon-
scious of our surroundings (strange as it may seem). We
could not keep up a 'Good heavens, skeletons!' attitude
all the time. But little episodes such as these happen
sometimes and make us for an instant register 'What
was that?'

The electric lighting has always been a trial to us. It
works, but it is temperamental. We have two stands;
one archaic and ponderous, the other aluminium and
angle-poised at apparently every joint. It depends entirely
on the temperament of the user which of the two is chosen
for work in the tombs. My own choice is for the heavy,
solid, uncompromising wooden one. There is about it an
obstinacy that I rather like. It seems to say: 'Here is your
light and here we stay.' But braver spirits try the streamlined modern gadget and are temerarious enough to
tamper with its half-dozen collapsing joints. One fixes
three, and the fourth brings the whole contraption down —
you know the sort of thing. And the generator's electric
current is just that touch too strong for its wiring; everything becomes unpleasantly hot and bulbs go 'pouff' and
flicker out at any moment. Electricians come and go and
pronounce it perfect, but it always wins.

Nancy, who refuses to be beaten by anything, was one
day enforcing her will upon this stand. She was photographing one of the excellent tombs containing undisturbed burials, when suddenly the tripod decided upon
revenge. As she gripped its middle to turn it yet a little
more, both it and she became alive with electricity.
Current at the rate of whatever it was pulsated through

her. Her hand was stuck to the wretched machine.
Ahmed, our foreman, was fortunately waiting in the shaft
and immediately crawled into the chamber in response to
her determined yelp for aid. He, poor chap, grabbed her
arm in a firm but uninitiated attempt at rescue. Alas, he
was instantly stuck to Nancy, and all three of them – the
tripod, Nancy, Ahmed – hopped about within the tomb,
jollied up with electricity. Nancy's proud boast later was

that they did not destroy a thing. But her dire thoughts
at the time were concentrated on shaking off Ahmed. It
was impossible to call for help – the generator drowned
all sound and contained enough petrol for another hour's
performance, and it and its controlling switch were at
the top of the shaft. With violent jerks Nancy interrupted
the *pas de trois*, hoping to rid herself of one or other of
the embracing menaces. At last poor Ahmed was shaken
free and she instructed him to leave the tomb and turn

off the current. Calm was restored, and in measured phrase sentence was passed upon the offending stand. Henceforth, until we can lure an electrician worthy of the name into our wilderness, we keep it only as an ornament, giving a specious air of efficiency to the Camp House.

The period of the Middle Bronze Age is the period of the Patriarchs, so we must remember that, while our Canaanites were flourishing in their strong citadels and trading with Egypt and enjoying the prosperity of the land, a little band headed by Abraham sallied forth from Ur of the Chaldees in Mesopotamia, and made its way into Palestine.

'Now the Lord had said unto Abraham – Go forth out of thy country, and from thy kindred and out of thy father's house, unto the land which I will show thee.' And Abraham took with him Sara his wife and a good sprinkling of relatives, and came into Canaan. There are vivid descriptions of them in Genesis, coming with their flocks and pitching their tents in the hill-country. We know from the contemporary Mari tablets that at this time donkeys were common, so most probably their beast of burden was that long-suffering animal.

Abraham and Sara visited Shechem and Hebron, towns whose walls of the period we still can see. Isaac was born to the aged pair and his home was in the hill-country above and to the south-west of Jericho. They feared that he might marry a Canaanite woman and be led astray from the promise of the Lord, so they sent back to their own people for a wife, and Rebecca was brought to Palestine for Isaac. Isaac's children, Esau and Jacob, prospered and became wealthy pastoralists. Jacob cheated poor furry Esau of his inheritance and received Isaac's blessing, and was then called Israel. It was to be from Jacob that the Children of Israel were to spring. We know that Jacob's son, Joseph, was sold by his brothers into captivity. This happened at Dothan, then a prosperous town like our Jericho, now a huge and desolate mound like Jericho.

Joseph was taken into Egypt, and in small bands his

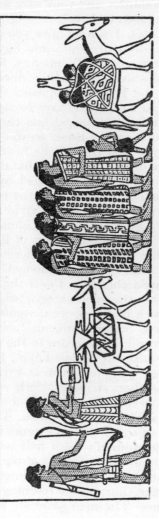

Asiatic visitors at Beni-Hasan

brothers and their wives and children, their servants and
their servants' wives followed him into the rich land to
the south – and they were known by the Egyptians as the
Children of Israel.

Alas, I cannot give you a date for the entry of the
Children of Israel into Egypt. Biblical scholars cannot
agree among themselves. Some like to think that the
semi-nomadic Semitic tribes entered Egypt in the wake
of the Hyksos conquerors when they overran Egypt in
1730 B.C. Others say: 'Nonsense, that is far too late; the
Semites infiltrated into the land of the Pharaohs at a
much earlier time.' So you see the difficulty. But let us
agree that the Middle Bronze Age of Palestine was the
age of the Patriarchs, that they lived humbly in the hill-
country uncontaminated by the prosperous life of our
Canaanite towns, and the best portrait of them that we
have comes from the vivid picture set up at Beni-Hasan
in Egypt, described so admirably by Dr Albright:

'The famous tableau of Beni-Hasan, dated in the year
1892 B.C., paints an unforgettable picture of a small clan
of semi-nomadic tribesmen from Palestine in the early
Patriarchal Age. Under the guidance of their chief, who
bears the good abbreviated Semitic name Absha, thirty-
seven of them, men, women, and children, are said to
have brought stibium (black pigment) from Shutu in
central Transjordan to the court of the monarch of the
district (in Middle Egypt, just north of Amarna). Both
men and women wear woollen tunics made by sewing
together strips of cloth woven in brightly coloured
patterns; these tunics are draped over one shoulder,
leaving the other bare. The only difference between
men's and women's tunics indicated by the artist is that
the women's reach half way between ankle and knee,
while the men's stop at the knee. However, some of the
men wear long white (linen?) tunics, and some of them
wear short tunics reaching only from the waist to the
knee. The men generally wear sandals, but the women
are shown wearing low leather boots. For weapons they
carry a composite bow, throw-sticks, and darts. The least-
expected items of luggage are a lyre carried by one of the

men and two bellows carried (with other things) by the
asses. Obviously we are dealing here with travelling
metal-workers, something like the tinkers of later times,
who were still a sufficient oddity in Egypt to be represented for posterity by the local prince. As a whole this
group perfectly illustrates the very ancient story in Gen.
iv, 19-22, where the family of Lamech is described as
including specialists in pastoral life, in playing the lyre,
and in copper and iron working. Since it is unlikely that
the dress of the Palestinian semi-nomad changed appre-
ciably in the following century or two, we can scarcely
go far wrong if we picture Jacob and his family as clad in
much the same way.'

W. F. Albright: *The Archaeology of Palestine* (Pelican
Books, 1954).

CHAPTER EIGHT

Joshua

(LATE BRONZE AGE: 1580-1200 B.C.)

ALTHOUGH Canaanite Palestine had prospered under its Hyksos overlords, Egypt had groaned, and the vassal states to the south of the Delta had waited for the day when they could turn upon the alien rulers, expel them from their capital at Avaris, and sweep them out of Egypt. At last that day came: a vassal king called Kamose revolted, and succeeded in expelling the foreign oppressors from Middle Egypt. Ahmose I, founder of the XVIIIth Dynasty, continued the attack and in 1580 B.C. captured Avaris and pursued the fleeing Hyksos into Palestine. The violence of the Egyptian retaliation can be seen today in the charred and blackened remains of the Middle Bronze Age towns and defences. One after another they were destroyed. At Tell Beit Mirsim and at Jericho, the destruction was overwhelming. In the small portion of the town that remains to us at Jericho we can see walls that have crashed down in flames. Even the grey mud bricks are scarlet and distorted. Panic there must have been, and flight from the town. It is possible to imagine the confusion at the gateway, the people pushing and jostling each other in their attempt to escape down the long ramp outside the walls on to the roads that led northwards up the Jordan Valley. Carrying what they could, these proud Middle Bronze Age people became refugees fleeing before the anger of the Egyptians, who kept the fires blazing in their town. Perhaps our Jerichoans, those who survived, found shelter farther north at Megiddo. This great city does not bear the marks of immediate destruction, and within its walls Canaanites of the Middle Bronze tradition continued to hold their own in a countryside laid waste and conquered by Egypt. For the

next four hundred years Palestine was a colony and paid
dearly for the privilege. The taxes were excessive and
often ruthlessly extracted. Egyptian columns and marks
of supremacy were set up in many of the towns, and
Beth-shan sheltered an Egyptian garrison. But the Late
Bronze Age people, as we now must call them, survived
the calamity. Slowly they crept back into many of the
ravaged towns, cleared the débris of destruction, and rebuilt. The pottery of the period shows clearly that the
traditions of the Middle Bronze Age continued, but at the
same time something new was added. At Megiddo, where
there was a continuous occupation from Middle to Late
Bronze Age, the later levels are characterized by new
forms of pottery decorated with lively little animals,
and birds and fishes, and there are pots with sweeping
geometric flamboyancies. At the same time too there are
imported vessels from Cyprus and the Eastern Mediterranean. But the folk remained faithful to the old ways,
and when a new gateway had to be built, they chose
the former Middle Bronze triple gateway as their model.

At Jericho the destruction had been too severe. Our
ancient town was once more deserted. Our people did not
go back. I remember once, when we were on the Tell,
the sky darkened to the south and our Arab workmen
pulled their headcloths round their faces and worked with
an apprehension that was infectious. They waited for the
dust storm that was sweeping up the Valley. The Dead
Sea gleamed below us as though it were made of polished
pewter, and a golden, luminous light suffused the Valley,
causing dimpling shadows on the hills of Moab across the
Jordan. It was very lovely, but the first fingers of the
wind rippled the loose earth on the Tell and soon the light
and the Dead Sea were obliterated, and we were en-
veloped in a cloud of dust.

The wind was not harsh with us to begin with; we
were just working in a still and secret world of ancient
mud mounds hidden from sight by a pall of dust. It was
difficult to see and breathe and the darkness became more
profound. For an hour we toiled on, and then at last the
winds lashed about us, carrying our dust too on and

upward to join the heavy cloud. It was impossible to work.
Our Arabs bound their faces almost completely and we
all turned our backs to the south. We waited like patient
animals for the Great Sitt to put an end to our futile
labours. Trenches, which a little before had been swept
and orderly, became filled with a grey and swirling
powder; all angles were turned to curves and sudden
gusts tore the coverings from fragile treasures we had
hoped to care for. Our own earth dumps were like smoking chimneys before the wind and we ourselves were
filled with sand. At last a messenger from the Great Sitt
told us all to stop. We covered up as best we could the
most precious of our 'finds' that still remained embedded
in the trenches, and thankfully made our way back to
the Camp House. Great drops of rain began to fall and
lay like coins in the dry dust. It then rained steadily all
night, and in the morning, although the air was clear,
our poor old mound was sheathed in mud. So it must
have been, winter after winter long ago, when the city
was deserted. There were no enthusiastic hands to clear
away the sticky earth as we did after our storm, to patch
up the damage or to fill in the widening gullies caused
by the rain. It must have been a sad sight, our deserted
town, as it sprawled there by the Spring, being blown
away by the winds and melting in the rains.

The fields and vineyards, too, will have suffered. It is
not only the prevailing wind that blows up from the
south, swarms of locusts follow the route of the Rift
Valley. They, too, darken the sky, and the villagers rush
out into their fields, flap their coats and arms, and mill
about. This is the simple man's primitive defence against
an age-old plague. As long as the locusts can be kept in
the air and on the move, all is well. At least 'All is well
for my field — heaven help my neighbours.' The locusts
can only fly for a certain length of time, and then they
must settle for rest and nourishment. They are silly,
bumbling, slow-flying creatures; hundreds fall by the
wayside, caught in our trenches and pits and holes, out
of which they seem to be quite incapable of flying. But
what are a few hundreds when a swarm consists of

millions? Nowadays there are special Government officials whose lives are devoted to the task of combating these pests: but when Jericho was deserted, no doubt they chose the peaceful green of the oasis for their resting place, and devoured the springing vegetation, reducing everything to wilderness.

Apart from the sounds of the ever-flowing water, silence descended upon Jericho for perhaps a hundred and fifty years. Situated to the east of Egypt's main trade route to the northern lands, it was forgotten. The hill towns to the west and those of the seaboard still flourished, but by degrees Egyptian plundering reduced their strength. We know that oxen, corn and slaves, gold and other treasures were taken, time and time again, into the greedy land of the Pharaohs. There was discontent and rebellion. Often these struggling Canaanite cities were destroyed. Megiddo bears the marks of three such catastrophes. And while the prosperity of Palestine was diminishing, the power and splendour of Egypt was ever increasing. Under the magnificent leadership of Thutmose III and, after him, Amenhotep III, the Empire dominated the neighbouring lands from Crete to the Euphrates.

When Amenhotep III died, he was followed by his son, a young man Amenhotep IV. He succeeded to the Empire and gods of his fathers, but the gods displeased him. He wished to praise one god only. He caused the old temples to be closed. The priests were cast out; and leaving the magnificent temple town of Thebes, with its multitudinous deities, he built his new capital at Amarna, farther down the Nile. To him Amen, the Theban god of the Empire, was now anathema. He changed his name from Amenhotep to Ikhnaton (meaning 'Aton, the Sun God, is satisfied'). The Sun god was to him the Creator of the Universe, the one and only God who loved all.

Thy beams encompass the lands to the sum of all that
    thou hast created,
Thou subduest them with thy love.

Thou quickenest the child in its mother's womb,
Thou soothest it that it cry not.

Then there is a chick within an egg, cheeping as it were
    within a stone,
Thou givest it breath therein to cause thy handiwork to
    live.

How excellent are thy ways, O Lord God of Eternity.

Such was his sublime hymn to Aton, the one and only
God. But the time was not ripe for such a vision. And
while he was building his palace and shrine to Aton at
Amarna, his Empire lacked guidance and control. The
soldiers were discontented, the priests of the old gods
hated the reform.

After his death, Tutankhamen, his son-in-law, rein-
stated the old religion and moved back to Thebes, and
Amarna fell into ruins. But in those ruins were buried
certain letters written on clay tablets. They are most
important because they give us a picture of the state of
the Empire. While Ikhnaton dreamed of a universal
love, the Hittites, invaders from Asia Minor using
weapons made of iron, were making inroads upon the
Empire in Syria. Palestine was in revolt and Egyptian
power was crumbling. In the Amarna letters we read of
desperate appeals from local governors for reinforcements,
appeals that are reiterated almost with despair. There
are accounts concerning local kings who have successfully
shaken off Imperial rule. And there are references to the
Habiru. These were warlike nomadic tribesfolk, whose
presence and infiltration was sufficiently felt for facts
about them to be recorded and sent back to the Imperial
capital at Amarna.

Who were these Habiru, whose activities were recorded
in letters dating between 1390 and 1365 B.C.? I like to
think with some others that possibly they were the
Hebrews of the Bible who, we know, made their great
Exodus from Egypt some time at least between 1400 and

1200 B.C. But it is all wretchedly difficult. Certain philologists say that the word 'Habiru' could mean 'Hebrew', and others say that it could not. Even those who say that the Habiru are the Hebrews complicate matters further by affirming that there are Northern Hebrews who became a menace, along with the Hittites, and must on no account be mistaken for the Children of Israel, who left Egypt and certainly made their presence felt within the Empire, coming in as they did from the eastern boundaries of Palestine. So you must realize that nothing is definite; there are scholars who say this and scholars who say that. The date of the Exodus and the name of the Pharaoh who suffered the various plagues at the hands of the Children of Israel, and who being so tormented eventually granted them permission to withdraw, is not known for certain. All we know is that at some period between 1400 and 1200, the Israelites left Egypt under Moses, as the Bible story tells us, and eventually established themselves in Palestine.

To me it is reasonable to suppose that the Habiru of the Amarna letters are the Hebrews of the Bible story. The accounts tally to a certain extent. The Bible tells us of the entry into Palestine and the fall of various cities to the victorious Israelites; the Amarna letters give accounts of the Habiru marauders and contain requests for reinforcements from governors who remained loyal to Egypt and wished to withstand the roving menace of the newcomers. And in 1230 the Pharaoh Merneptah records that he vanquished the 'people of Israel' – which presupposes there were people of Israel established in Palestine by that time. But if we like to think that these Habiru are the Hebrews, we cannot have them going into Egypt in the wake of the Hyksos invaders in the eighteenth century B.C., because then they would not have had time to have spent their four hundred and thirty years in Egypt as the Bible tells us they did. On the other hand, if you prefer to take them in with the Hyksos, then you must bring them out again four hundred and thirty years later and make Rameses II the Pharaoh of the oppression. Or perhaps the biblical estimate of four hundred and thirty years need not be taken too literally. It is all unproven and we may think as we please.

But to return to Jericho, some time about the year 1400 B.C., a few of the Late Bronze Age people rediscovered the forgotten mound by the Spring and they returned to it, perhaps enticed by the generosity of the fresh water as it flowed continuously there in the desert. They must have built a settlement and assuredly there will have been walls about it, although all trace of them has been washed away. Certain of their tombs have been found containing pottery (none earlier than 1400) and we have found a small portion of one of their dwellings upon the Tell. On the eastern slope of the mound a floor and hearth and one pot are evidence, meagre enough admittedly, of the town which Joshua saw as he rested on the far side of the Jordan preparatory to his entry into the Land of the Promise. The fact that one pot was still there and that the few tombs were there is evidence enough of the settlement that he overcame.

The Bible story tells us that a little before this time Moses assumed leadership of the people of Israel, and they sought permission from Pharaoh to leave the country. But it was not granted till later, after ten plagues had made the Egyptian tyrants more amenable. After the last and most terrible plague there was 'a great cry throughout all the land of Egypt' at the death of the firstborn, and the Pharaoh bade the Israelites depart. Later, regretting his decision, he pursued Moses and his people to the shores of the Red Sea. The waters overwhelmed his army and his chariots; the Hebrews passed unscathed through the waters and eventually came to Sinai, where, we are told, Moses ascended the mountain on numerous occasions to speak with the Lord. He received the Ten Commandments, and the Book of the Covenant came into being as the earliest Israelitish code of laws. There followed a period of wandering in the wilderness, until eventually Moses led his people into Moab on the east side of the Jordan, and there he died within sight of the Promised Land.

Joshua during all this time had proved himself to be a

loyal supporter of his leader. In spite of all the difficulties and disappointments, he had shown an ardent faith in Jehovah and in the destiny of the Children of Israel. He became the commander.

You must imagine them encamped at the foot of the mountains to the east of the Jordan river. They have looked across the Valley and seen Jericho situated at the base of the towering heights that we now know as the Hills of Judah. They have seen the putty-coloured desert, broken only by the dark tamarisk groves on the banks of the Jordan, and beyond, the brilliant green fields round Jericho. They had to cross the river and take the town. Joshua commanded the people to prepare foodstuffs, for in three days they would pass over the Jordan and enter into the land promised to them by God. The Bible records that Joshua sent two spies across the river who were to 'view the land, even Jericho'. The spies made their way into the town and soon their presence was reported to the King because the people of Canaan were in great fear of the invading Israelites. The King sent messengers to apprehend the spies, and Rahab, ' the harlot of Jericho', hid them in her house. A search was instituted for them, and Rahab let them down from her house 'on the wall' in a basket, and told them to hide in the neighbouring mountains until the search should be over, and later to cross the river and return to Joshua. For saving their lives thus, she requested that when the Israelites attacked, her life and that of her mother, father and family should be spared: this the Hebrews promised. And so that they should know whom to spare, they instructed her to tie a red cord to her window, so that all within her house should be saved. In due course the spies returned to Joshua's encampment and reported all that had passed. The following day Joshua led his people to the brink of the Jordan and the Bible relates that miraculously the waters piled up and the Israelites, bearing the Ark of the Covenant, passed over the River. One from each of the twelve tribes took a stone and set it up as a memorial marking the spot where 'the waters of the Jordan were cut off before the Ark of the Covenant of the Lord'. After

E

the passage of all the people 'the waters of the Jordan returned to their place'.

Professor Garstang writes: 'People trained to scientific thought today are not disposed to believe in the possibility of any phenomenon which defies the laws of human experience'; and so he suggests that, on the occasion of the crossing, the river might have been blocked by a landslide. Several of these landslides are on record. 'The earliest record dates from A.D. 1266, when the Sultan Bibars ordered a bridge to be built across the Jordan in the neighbourhood of Damieh. The task was found to be difficult owing to the rise of the waters. But in the night preceding the 8th December, 1267, a lofty mound, which overlooked the river on the West, fell into it and dammed it up so that the water of the river ceased to flow and none remained in its bed. The waters spread over the valley above the dam and none flowed down the bed for some sixteen hours. There was another similar occurrence about the year 1906, and the most recent was during the earthquakes of 1927 ... and no water flowed down the river bed for twenty-one hours.'[1]

By this time, and most naturally, fear had entered into the hearts of our poor Jerichoans. They were isolated in the Valley and at the mercy of the advancing horde. Egypt would not have listened to an appeal. Her only interest lay in keeping the northern trade route open, and Jericho was too peripheral even to be considered. The townsmen shut their gates. The Bible story gives us no indication that any of them was man enough to come out and fight. Joshua formed up his warriors and behind them came seven priests and the Ark of the Covenant. Every priest had a ram's horn trumpet upon which he was to blow loudly all the time. And once each day for six days this procession passed round the city at the foot of the walls, and on the seventh day they all rose early and 'compassed the city after the same manner seven times'. My heart bleeds for the unfortunate and somewhat cowardly Jerichoans. Their morale must have been reduced considerably by the pressure of this cold war tactic.

[1] John Garstang, *Joshua, Judges* (London, 1931).

Then Joshua commanded the priests to blow yet again on the trumpets, and he bade all the people to shout, and he cursed all in the miserable city, all except Rahab the harlot and those with her in her house. And as the priests trumpeted and the people shouted, the 'wall fell down flat'.

Those of you who wish can affirm that 'an earthquake brought the walls down', and of course there is no one to deny it. But to me it is wonderful that an opportune earthquake should have shaken the Valley at that particular moment. Then the Israelites rushed up and took the city, and they utterly destroyed all that was in it 'both man and woman, young and old, and ox, sheep and ass with the edge of the sword'. This I think was perhaps going a little bit too far, but we must remember that it all occurred over three thousand years ago, and standards change (or do they?). The two spies sought Rahab in her house and they led her forth into safety with her father and her family, and she dwelt happily with the Israelites.

But Joshua had not finished with Jericho. He caused it to be burnt and laid a curse upon it that it should not be rebuilt. And then the Israelites pushed onward into the hill country, leaving the town ravaged and beaten in the Valley. Thereafter time dealt even more drastically with it than had Joshua's trumpets; for today the solitary floor of which I have spoken is the only relic of that epoch.

While we were digging in the cemetery area we were always hoping to find Late Bronze Age tombs of, or about, the time of Joshua. The few that there are were found before our own excavations. Each time as the shafts were cleared we would say hopefully to one another: 'Perhaps this time we shall succeed.' But as our men heaved back a door slab we would find another of our old friends of the Middle Bronze or earlier.

Nevertheless, our search goes on, and in our fossickings round the Arab Refugee Village, although disappointed at not finding later tombs, we have come across many a delightful character among the Refugees. There is the baker on the Muddy Wadi Street. His shop lies on one of our tracks through the village. It consists of a small room with a beaten mud floor. The room is open wide at one end to the street, and at the other the baker stands in a hole in the floor, beyond which is his oven. He keeps a crackling fire of burning sticks in the oven on the left hand side; the flames curl up and round the roof. To the right he puts the dough. The women bring their unbaked bread to him, and squat about the floor and chatter while he flips the loaves in and out of his oven. He has an art of flicking the dough about with a long wooden spatula. He will turn over three, put in a fourth, and bring out five, six and seven with an easy turn of the wrist. His timing is perfect: none ever seems to burn.

I first encountered him as I made my way to a new shaft beyond his establishment. 'Oh that it be Late

Bronze' ran my thoughts, when 'Salaam aleikum' assailed my ears. I stopped at his doorway and returned his good wishes. For one moment I hesitated, and then I stepped in. Ten veils were pulled round averted faces and only my cheery baker looked up at me from his hole in the floor. Having crashed in upon them thus, I determined to see the encounter through and wished the anti-social ladies 'Good morning'. A few appeared to mellow and the baker was delighted. He was entirely master of the situation and bade me jump into the hole and look into his oven. I pronounced everything good; I think I said 'good' twice to make certain that everyone realized I thought it an excellent bakery; and out I scrambled. One of the women

offered me some of her freshly baked bread, and I said
'Good' again and smiled. The ice was broken and we
were well away. I even squatted on the floor and was
persuaded to eat a bit of an apple turnover. It was so
hot that I blistered my mouth, but I managed to keep
smiling. The baker beamed upon us all. After that day
I always called to see him and his assorted housewives.
I was accepted.

Indeed Diana and I have been lucky enough to be
entirely accepted by the village. We are asked in to see
the new baby, usually a tiny overdecorated bambino.
The swaddling clothes are wrapped so tightly, one won-
ders how it ever breathes. It lies, an inert bundle, in a
plywood box on rockers. There are tiny beads tied to its
wisps of hair, and its eyes are smeared with some peculiar
black stuff which is supposed to keep the flies away, but
which, in fact, seems to attract them all the more.

We stand solemnly with the crowd as a funeral procession makes its way up our road and passes to the low
ridge beyond the village. Here the twentieth-century
dead are buried in much shallower graves than any that
we are used to, and with much greater simplicity. But
no doubt the cortège is just the same: the wailing, lament-
ing women, the steady march of the men who carry the
corpse swathed in white and held aloft, and the running
children.

And we are asked to weddings. Being women from
another planet we are allowed to mix with both halves of
the strictly segregated party. The bridegroom sits in self-
conscious state on two mattresses outside in the courtyard.
Round him in an admiring throng stand or squat all the
male relatives who can force their way into the small
enclosure. Sporadic conversation occurs among the guests,
and cigarettes are smoked. Usually an evening breeze
gets up, and it can be chilly and a little dusty. We, who
are seated on two stools beside the bridegroom, decide to
visit the ladies. As we rise, everybody pushes somebody
out of our way and we proceed fifteen paces to the door
of the one-roomed house that is to be the house of the
newly married pair. The brother of the bridegroom forces

his way through the almost solid mass of women. He even hauls out four or five to relieve the congestion and we are led to the bride. Our two stools are passed over fifty heads and placed near her. We say 'Lovely' and smile. Her eyes are cast down. She is too faint through lack of oxygen to move. Perspiration streams down every gleaming face. Drums are beating, and in the one spare square foot of floor, a guest is dancing. It is the wonder-

ful tummy-wobble dance of the Orient. I do not know how they do it. A wobble begins at the shoulders, shudders there for a moment or two and then settles in the hips, only to fade away as it begins at the shoulders again.

On one occasion I was called upon to dance at one of these women's parties. I knew I could not compete with this tummy-wobble business. I had tried it in private and admitted to myself that I was neither physically nor spiritually suited to such a performance. But I knew they wanted movement; unfortunately I was never taught Greek eurhythmics, so, perforce, I gave them the Charleston. Half way through my rendering they threw a veil over my head. I was very grateful to whichever one of them had done so kind a deed; it is not nearly so bad Charlestoning alone in a packed room if your head is covered.

Diana and I wait at these indoor celebrations until we find it difficult to breathe and then we are passed out into the night: we leave the wedding party – an island of flaring oil lamps and merry hullabaloo in the sleeping, dark village. Our road leads us along the foot of the Tell, which rises black and towering on our right. In the distance the electric lamps of modern Jericho gleam among the palm trees, and far away to the east across the Valley a tiny group of lights, clustered like the Pleiades, tells us that the villagers of Shuni have not yet gone to sleep. This little village stands at the foot of the ravine that leads down from the heights of Moab, and it must have been from somewhere near those lights that Moses and Joshua looked across the Jordan and saw Jericho.

CHAPTER NINE

The End

THE IRON AGE: 1200-588 B.C.

WHILE the Hebrews were pushing into the hills of Palestine and overcoming the weaker of the Canaanite towns, the old Aegean civilization of the Eastern Mediterranean was enjoying the last decades of its greatness. Soon it was to crumble before invasion and then Aegean refugees made their way southwards and eastwards. Although repulsed by the Egyptians they managed to gain a place for themselves on the southern Levant seaboard: thenceforward they were known as Philistines, whence the modern name Palestine. Their new home lay in the fertile plain between the sea and the hills, where they founded a series of strong city states.

In the meantime the Hebrews in the hill country were adapting themselves to the local Canaanite ways of life. They came to Palestine as shepherd nomads, but by degrees they mingled with the older inhabitants, trading with them and imitating their manners and customs. This is a formative period in the history of the Children of Israel, and their destiny was guided by leaders, known as Judges, who constantly thundered at them when they were led too far astray by temptations offered by the easier way of Canaanite living, or when they fell, as they so often did, into the worship of the local gods. But nevertheless a national consciousness was developing among them, despite the differences between the north and south of the country. Life was richer and more settled in the north; but in the south, in the arid Hills of Judah, the Hebrews retained longer their roving disposition. As yet they had failed to conquer Ophel, the old Jerusalem, and they were not in possession of any important centre.

It was to their advantage that the power of Egypt was waning. After Rameses III, 1198-1167 B.C., eight more Pharaohs, all called Rameses, succeeded one another; not one of them was able to regain control of Palestine. But to the west the newly settled Philistines were beginning to extend their frontiers. About the year 1150 B.C., Megiddo, the great stronghold of Late Bronze Canaan, was overwhelmed: it is thought that this destruction was brought about by the Philistines. Many of the other towns of Western Palestine bear the marks of devastation at this period, and from the Bible we know that the Israelites were conquered, the town of Shiloh destroyed and the Ark of the Covenant captured.

In 1020 B.C., Saul led a revolt and succeeded for some time in throwing off the Philistine yoke; but it was not until the reign of David (c. 990 B.C.) that the Hebrews were able to establish a kingdom. David captured Jerusalem and built his city there. For seventy-five years this small united kingdom of the northern tribes and the southern was a power in Western Asia. The Philistines withdrew to the coastal strip, and David, followed by Solomon, ruled a kingdom which extended as far north as Damascus.

By degrees the Canaanites were absorbed and their towns taken over by the people of the kingdom. The new pottery and houses were crude by comparison with what had gone before, but under the reign of Solomon there was a flowering of material civilization. The Bible paints a vivid picture of the wealth and luxury of those days. We are told how the King sent his merchants and his craftsmen far and wide to procure the rare materials for his buildings. Remains of the copper refineries in the Wadi Arabah and smelting furnaces near the Gulf of Akaba are all that exist now to tell us of the enterprise of Solomon's craftsmen. But certainly in the building of his palace and his great temple at Jerusalem he must have stimulated artistic development and encouraged trade with the neighbouring states.

At Jericho, our expedition has found just one tomb belonging to this period. It is a shafted chamber in the

E*

main cemetery area and is dated approximately the tenth century B.C. As yet we have found no trace of dwellings on or near the Tell belonging to this early Iron Age time. Maybe some families sought asylum in the Valley and made an encampment by the Spring, for the luxuries of Solomon and his court must have placed a heavy burden on the people. So much so, in fact, that shortly after the death of the King, Jeroboam revolted and the Kingdom was divided. Jeroboam ruled Israel in the north, consisting of ten of the tribes, and Rehoboam, Solomon's son, reigned in Jerusalem over the tribes of Benjamin and Judah.

In 880 B.C., Omri, King of the North, moved his capital from Tirzah and founded the city of Samaria. The Bible tells us that one after another these northern kings 'provoked the Lord God of Israel', and the worst of all was Ahab, Omri's son. Ahab worshipped Baal and 'in his days did Hiel the Bethelite build Jericho'. Remember Joshua had cursed Jericho that none should rebuild it – and here was Hiel the Bethelite rebuilding.

On the Tell we have in fact found buildings only a little later in date than Hiel the Bethelite. They lie at the outer end of our main trench, built over débris that had cascaded down the slope of the Middle Bronze Age defences, but they do not tell us much except that they are there. Our trench cuts through the foundations and mud-brick walls of various buildings that have sprawled out on to the natural rock beyond the limits of the ancient mound. It may have been to this settlement that Elijah came before he made his way up the brook Kerith to shelter in one of the rocky caves in the steep sides of the Wadi Kelt, a ravine which runs from the mountains into the Valley below Jericho. This is a favourite walk of ours on Sundays.

All through the week we busily discuss plans for the coming Sunday. The pros and cons of this and that expedition are carefully studied. We can rattle off in the 'dig' car to the wonderful remains of the Roman city of Jerash, or drive through the hills to Omri's ancient capital at Samaria. Local buses struggle up the steep winding

road to Jerusalem each day; on Sunday you will find a
few of us wedged in among the solemn locals. But if our
wish is to escape from bustle and people, there is nothing
better than the long tramp down the Wadi Kelt.

On Sunday mornings I go to our small church at
Jericho and it impresses me vividly each time. I cannot
help thinking how much the Lord must smile at our
endeavours. On either side of the front door are two
Gordon's Gin bottles upside down dripping holy water
into saucers. Our Italian priest is very practical, and no
doubt too much holy water evaporated in the scorching
heat in the days before the Gordon's Gin bottles. We
lift a heavy curtain as we enter and go into the cool and
whitewashed church. I know the drill now, women on
the left, men on the right and babies in the aisle, so I
hesitate at the door to allow the eyes to become acclima-
tized. It is so easy to trip over crawling bodies in the aisle.
At first it seems difficult to find a place in the women's
benches: I used to panic a little at the thought that I
would have to horrify *everyone* and push in among the
men; but fortunately I have always managed to squeeze
in somewhere and usually find myself passed along to
about the middle of a bench where I am wedged in between enormous peasant women in full regalia. On the
other side of the aisle the men are also tightly jammed:
Arab Legionaries, fat old merchants, skinny youths —
each one of them, I should say, a Papa judging by the
to'ing and fro'ing of the children in the aisle. This segre-
gation is not a good arrangement, either for silence or
order, because the babies spend their time making sorties
from Mamma, in the women's benches, and burrowing
through the men until they find Papa. They will pass
a few moments with that distracted parent before burrowing out again. This occupation is interspersed with exploratory excursions up and down the aisle. There was
one little fellow aged about three who mostly favoured
the aisle; he was dressed in a complete Franciscan habit
and pottered up and down all through the sermon rattling
his rosary beads, looking like a miniature St Francis.
The hymns are sung with a deafening gusto. The object

of the singing seems to be that you should sing louder than your neighbour and make it as nasal as you can. While I was desperately concentrating, and attempting to read the Gospel for the Fifth Sunday after the Epiphany, suddenly St Francis fell over, and the whole of our bench became upheaved as a bigger sister was passed out along the line of women to rescue him. Then at last we hear the rather tired Italian priest say Ite Missa Est, and we all pour out into the blinding sunshine.

I well remember one Sunday when Dorothy and I planned to make the long walk down the Wadi Kelt. After breakfast we set off from the Camp House carrying our sandwiches and bathing suits. A mile of dusty road separated us from the main square of modern Jericho, but we marched along the road at ease, returning the salutes of many of our workmen who were clustered in aimless groups along the route, and were quite unrecognizable in their cleaner clothes and spotless head cloths. Our road leads us past banana groves and small natty stone villas belonging to the wealthy merchants from Jerusalem, who have found that it is pleasant to escape at weekends from the cold heights of the Judaean hills into the perfect winter climate of the Valley. Everywhere there are palms, oranges, bougainvillaea and bananas, and in the midst of this beautiful oasis is the busy heart of the little town.

Here, trade is carried on in the most satisfactory manner. The owner drapes all his wares on to his shop front and then sits inside in the shade, drinking innumerable cups of sweet black tea with potential buyers. Time is of no consequence and the acceptance of at least two cigarettes is *de rigueur*.

Dorothy and I seated ourselves in the battered grey bus which leaves, when it is full, for Jerusalem. Bedu women, smart Europeanized clerks and peasants piled in all round us, and at last we set out along the Valley and moved up into the hills. The ascent to Jerusalem is divided by a small plateau. The road winds up and up through the limestone hills and then debouches on to the plateau, which it traverses until the last steep ascent carries one finally upwards to the city, which is about three thousand five hundred feet above Jericho.

On this occasion, Dorothy and I left the bus before it crossed the plateau and followed a goat track into the ravine of the Wadi Kelt. We struck the stream just below a waterfall: it was our intention to bathe in the pool below the fall and have lunch on the warm rocks before we began the descent to Jericho. We were a trifle disconcerted when a roving goatherd attached himself to us. Often these wild, dagger-bedecked and picturesque creatures will march along with one for miles. They sit when we sit and move on when we do, keeping a distance of about twenty yards from us all the time. Normally we would have had no objection to his shadowing presence, but on this day we wished to bathe, and scantily clad women are anathema to Allah and to Mohammedan goatherds. At the pool two dusky youths, clad in singlets and shorts, were wading about with fishing nets, catching tiddlers. We were downcast: it would be impossible to shake off three gentlemen all based on the pool; we thought we would only be able to paddle. At this moment one of the shrimpers immersed himself in the clear enticing water, and said to us in hesitant English that it was an ideal place for a bathe. We told him our tale and indicated the goatherd, whereupon he announced that he himself was an Armenian Christian, completely shockproof, and understood perfectly. He would rid us of this wild Mussulman. A long colloquy ensued: he reported that he had told the goatherd that the Christian ladies desired to bathe and that they had no wish to offend his eyes, so would he be kind enough to withdraw. This the obliging youth proceeded to do, and we performed miracles of modesty behind a microscopic rock and emerged in our bathing suits. No sooner were we in the water, with our Armenian Christian and understanding friends, than the Muslim goatherd reappeared, flitting like Ben Gunn from rock to rock, until he found a position satisfactory to himself with the pool in his direct line of vision. We felt we could do no more: he had been warned. Later we changed and had our lunch, with Ben Gunn sitting twenty yards away and watching each mouthful. We gave him a tomato and he seemed very pleased.

It was time for us to move on. There were five miles to go down the ravine to Jericho, and the way follows the stream which flows not in its bed at the foot of the Wadi, but in a channel originally constructed by Roman engineers. The aqueduct is cut into the steep rocky side of the gorge and winds gently downhill all the way. At times the barren hills tower above it, and always the drop into the ravine is terrifying. Occasionally a shepherd's pipe is heard and the tinkling of sheep bells, and on all sides we are closed in with wilderness. The sun was warm on our backs. It was only when we rested after an hour or so that we discovered that Ben Gunn was still with us.

Sometimes the channel is carried across tributary ravines on great spindly concrete struts, and we had to wade along in the swiftly flowing water with a forty foot drop on either side. On and down we went until at last we came to the water-chute. At this point the channel ceases and the stream cascades into the bed of the gorge one hundred and fifty feet below. Here one can clamber down beside the fall, to follow the channel again on the other side of the ravine; but an alternative way leads through the Monastery. This Monastery is built against the side of the Wadi with sheer rocks above and below it. Here, traditionally the site of Elijah's hermitage, holy men have made their abode. The rock face is studded with cells, and for many centuries now monks have lived and prayed here in spite of siege, devastation and indifference.

We marched along the track on a narrow ledge. In front of us was the huge and forbidding door. Perched out on projecting supports, the small church with its sky-blue dome seemed to hang in the air above the stream so far below. We boldly hauled at the bell-pull, and at the same time espied Ben Gunn scrambling down into the gorge. We waited. It was not the sort of bell one could control and we were fearful of reawakening the harsh iron clangings that echoed and re-echoed from the rocks. But three pulls were necessary before the door was slowly dragged back and a dear old wizened monk bade us enter.

There are a number of these small Greek Orthodox
monasteries suspended on the rocky slopes of the Palestinian hills. In each, four or five monks are all that remain of communities that have at times been composed
of hundreds. Nevertheless the tradition of hospitality has
survived. The traveller who is strong enough to go on
hauling at the bell-pull is in the end sure of refreshment
and rest. Dorothy and I were made welcome on a balcony
looking out over the ravine; tiny cups of black sweetened
tea were brought to us, and one of the monks who spoke
a little French told us about the inmates and the
Monastery.

'Brother Theodosius has been here for forty years,' he
told us, indicating a black bundle at the other end of the
bench.

Our eyes immediately turned to Brother Theodosius:
his kindly watery eyes beamed back at us and he nodded
his head so violently that the hairpins nearly fell out of
the prescribed bun of snowy locks hanging loosely at the
nape of his neck.

Forty years in the Wadi Kelt! We felt we were indeed
in the presence of an anchorite. With their black robes
flowing round them the monks led us to the Church,
which, for all its gleaming outside, was dark and candle-
lit, and filled with witch balls, as is the custom, and
not-very-good ikons. Then they took us to the lower
gate and blessed us on our way.

Ben Gunn was waiting. What could he want? We
were a little mystified by his devotion. We tramped on for
two more hours. Gradually the ravine merged into the
Jordan Valley, and away to our left we could see the Tell
and the palm trees round the spring and the Camp House.
It was dusk as we approached the House, and Ben Gunn
for the first time became articulate. We had no idea what
he was trying to say, but, whatever it was, it was
obviously most important. He still retained his distance
and his respect, but he spoke with determined earnestness. We called the cook: he would interpret for us. And
then it was that the reason for that long tramp became
apparent. Could we give him work? He was a goatherd

without goats, he was strong, he was young, he was willing. We stood there aghast; poor fellow—a whole day
had been given to that forlorn hope. He looked at us as
Ben Gunn must have looked at the retreating ship that had
marooned him. No, there was no work. He understood
and quickly disappeared into the half light, back into
the hills that were his home. We had no time even to
give him a little money, and sadly we turned to the glowing warmth of the Camp and to drinks and friends and
dinner.

Sunday evening chatter round our dining table has a
different flavour from other days. It is inevitably tinged
with reminiscence of the day's outing. There are those
who have been to Jerusalem and want to tell us every
detail; those who have been to the Dead Sea, and so on.
But the few, usually the botanists, who have been to the
landslide make us all vocal. A few years ago on the road
to Amman, on the very prettiest part of the way where
the flowers grow in profusion, the road and an adjoining
field slithered down the slope and came to rest upon a
field below. From that day to this there have been law
suits and appeals and more law suits over the ownership
of the land. The fellow below says it is his, since that is
where his field was, and the fellow above claims it as his
own, since the actual clay and rubble of the surface was the
clay and rubble of his ploughing. It has not been settled
yet. The few who tell us, on a Sunday evening, that they
have been to the landslide wish to tell us of the rare
flowers they have collected; but they find themselves
instead aiding and abetting the quasi-legal discussion
that ensues. It seems to me that many a time we have
finally settled the problem, but both we and the Jordan
magistrates find ourselves discussing it with renewed
vigour whenever it crops up.

By degrees, as the days of the excavation become numbered, a momentous thing called The Division looms on
the horizon, colouring all our activities, thoughts, deeds.
It consists of a visitation from Mr Lankester Harding,
who comes down from Amman to select from among our
treasures all those which he thinks should remain in the

possession of the Jordanian people. This is Mr Harding's first appearance in the present story: but he is in fact the *deus ex machina* throughout the whole work. Officially he is the Head of the Antiquities Department of the Hashemite Kingdom of Jordan, but to us he is a very great deal more than that. His weekly visits are occasions in which archaeology is not always the dominant motif. But now his advent is a solemn and momentous one, and the days preceding are a nightmare. Work in every department is speeded up so that as many objects as possible from the season's work are drawn, photographed and recorded in readiness for the selection.

In the 'good old days' the finds from archaeological expeditions were divided into two lots by the experts who had conducted and financed the excavations, and to ensure an absolutely even distribution, the first choice was given to the representatives of the country of origin. This was a wonderfully fair way of dividing the spoil: no one in their senses would make one lot contain all the plums if the other side had first choice. But this simple method has vanished, and we all have to consider ourselves very lucky now to be given anything whatever; in fact, we must consider ourselves lucky to be given permission to excavate at all. So when Mr Harding arrives we await the verdict with a certain anxiety. Treasures are necessary to *us* too, because we have to satisfy hungry museums and universities all over the world who have financed our endeavours. Their generosity is for the high ideal of knowledge, we know; but few of them exist in such a rarefied atmosphere that they do not respond to material returns. A good tomb group, or a Neolithic plastered skull, is an aid to generosity. You can imagine what our gloom would be if Mr Harding decided that all our plums must stay in Jordan; but in fact we and Jordan are satisfied after each Division. We take the bulk and Jordan keeps the unique finds. But in our bulk there are many exquisite things, and all that we take has to be carefully packed and shipped to various corners of the world.

The people in the Conservation Department are desperately overworked. Everything must leave the

Expedition House strong enough to withstand the long journey. More and more trays appear, trays filled with bones, baskets, wooden objects, and all needing attention. Poor Cecil, who rules like a sometimes benevolent despot in her department, marshals her slaves and sets us all to work. We paint strengthening solution on so many lower jaws that it is unbelievable that anybody could want so many; but anthropologists must have hundreds. So jaws with one tooth, two teeth, ten, fifteen, big jaws, little jaws, all from our Pre-pottery Neolithic levels, are impregnated and lie hardening in trays. Lines and lines of brittle baskets are slowly hardened with melted wax. Out of the context of their tombs they are poor things, though remarkable. And of course there is pottery – oh, preserve me from broken pots! Bits and pieces lie sprawled about the table in heart-rending disarray. I loathe jig-saw puzzles, and one must have the puzzle turn of mind in order to become a successful pot mender. Cecil has no mercy on us. If pots are to be mended, there we sit in the evenings mending them. I would look longingly at jaws, and even at the not-so-precious bits of wood that we amateurs were allowed to strengthen; but no, we had to do one pot per person before we were promoted to familiar, friendly bones.

Often she would produce a bottle from her shelves and we would note that it was not labelled acetone or vinamul but bore the cheering label, brandy. I remember one evening there were three of us left in the conservation room and it lacked ten minutes to eleven p.m., the hour when the generator is switched off and the electric lights go out. We lighted a last cigarette and poured ourselves a brandy. The table at which I had been working was so fully laden that there was no space even for one small glass, and perforce I had to put it on a tray which held the thigh bones of a Middle Bronze Age Jerichoan. One or two dead flies shared the tray; they had fallen there, stricken by the morning's D.D.T. spray. I looked across at Cecil and Nancy seated on their orange boxes under the harsh light, their elbows resting near the decayed remains of antique baskets, human bones and pottery. Perhaps it *was* a Grand Guignol after all? I felt compelled to tell them of a wonderful idea I had had. How would it be, I asked, if the B.B.C. recorded the noises from a tomb? It would have to be speeded up of course, much as the films give one the opening of a rose. My plan would telescope the sound of centuries into five or ten minutes. We would begin with the noises of the burial, the weeping women, the muffled thud as the corpse was laid on the floor, and the rattle of the pottery gifts as they were placed about; then the heaving of the rock door as it was pushed into position. There would be faint thuds and scrapings as the earth was filled in behind it; then a nice dramatic silence for a little, representing who knows how many years; and next, 'ping', as the ligaments holding the jaw disintegrated and allowed it to fall with a rattle on to the chest. There would be the clatter of the hand-bones as they dropped through the rib-case; an earth tremor would bring a small lump of ceiling down; the wooden legs of the table would collapse and the dishes scatter. More silence, more earth tremors and the lamp in its niche could fall with a crash. I was warming to the theme when the lights went out. . . .

Back on the Tell, towards the end of the 'dig', a slight anxiety can be sensed among the workmen. They know from experience that work in some of the trenches ceases before that in others, and they hope with a quiet intensity that their particular trench is of supreme importance, and therefore will not be one of those to be closed first. They have even been known to work harder and better in the hope that the smoothness of their performance can influence the decision. I suppose, too, in the back of their minds they feel it is good to leave a favourable impression, so that the Great Sitt may want to employ them again the following season. On the whole, our team consists of the same group of men each season: we get to know their worth and their peccadilloes. One man, who works on the Iron Age part of the Main Trench, answers to the name of Telephone. Some wit christened him this because of his unending salutation 'Hallo, hallo', and the name has stuck.

As I have said, the Iron Age settlement is cut a little way into the mound and sprawls out on to the natural rock to the west. On the whole it is the most unspectacular group of buildings and is covered by rubbish washed down from the earlier town above. We have found two tombs, one of which contained pottery datable to the seventh century B.C., which shows that our greatly reduced Jericho in the Southern Kingdom of Judah was still extant while the unfortunate Hebrews of the Northern Kingdom of Israel were being mercilessly handled by the Assyrian invaders from the northeast.

First in 734 B.C. the north was attacked and most of the kingdom was lost, and in 720 B.C. when Sargon invaded, Israel ceased to exist as an entity. Many of the inhabitants were taken into slavery and the ten tribes of Israel were lost to history.

The frontiers of Judah, the Southern Kingdom of the tribes of Benjamin and Judah, were now exposed to the peril of Assyrian attack, nor was it long before Sennacherib invaded and ravaged the land. Judah survived for another century as a vassal state; but throughout this period Jerusalem did not fall to the Assyrians and Hezekiah strengthened the city.

In Judah alone, now, were the national hopes of the Hebrews centred. But the Babylonians overwhelmed the Assyrians, and in 589 B.C. Nebuchadnezzar annexed Judah. The leaders of the Hebrew people were taken into captivity and many of the towns were sacked, among them Jerusalem, where the great Temple of Solomon was destroyed. The Bible story tells us that Zedekiah the King of Judah, having taken one look at the terrifying might of Nebuchadnezzar's army as it surrounded Jerusalem, fled from the city. He fled to the 'plains of Jericho'. He cannot have hoped for protection in the meagre settlement beside the ancient mound, but he sought refuge in the lonely wilderness about our town. It was of no avail. The Babylonian army pursued him and the nobles and men who had fled with him, and they brought them back to Nebuchadnezzar. Many of them were slaughtered, and Zedekiah's eyes were put out; he was then bound in chains and carried into captivity.

With most of the towns destroyed and the countryside depopulated by the Babylonians, Palestine was in a poor way. The people who remained eked out an existence in village settlements, and there are no buildings worthy of record in the length and breadth of the land. Jericho was deserted, the Spring waters flowed uncontrolled. At last, after more than five thousand years, the old town was forgotten.

CHAPTER TEN

Packing up

TWO celebrations occur before the end of the 'dig': one is the party that our Arab workmen give to us, and the other the party given to our Arab workmen by the Great Sitt.

Theirs consists of a wonderful song and dance called a fantasia, and the Jericho fantasia is renowned. Even the 1897 Baedeker in the bookshelves at the Camp House, having warned the intrepid traveller against the likelihood of 'Gyppy tummy', mosquitoes, heat and dust to be encountered at Jericho, is gracious enough to refer to this local fantasia, and advises the traveller to command a performance at the cost of a few *fils*. But we are lucky enough to attend a performance which is offered from *joie de vivre*, from gratitude, and from hope of more good things to come. Nominally it begins at 8 p.m., after our dinner, but from about five o'clock onwards our Camp House island between the channels from the Spring becomes a battle ground. The battle is waged between about three hundred men and Saleh, our dig foreman, who, with a huge stick, intends to keep a space of earth free of bodies for the dancers and the singers. While he beats shoulders and ankles at one side of the circle, the crowd encroaches on the other. He rushes like a goaded bull to the other side and belabours there. I often wonder why he does it because it must be most exhausting, and always he is the loser.

At eight we all appear muffled to our ears in coats and rugs. Although the days are hot, the evenings are still cold and, as loyal spectators, our task is to sit perched up on the Camp House wall until the last dancer drops exhausted at an hour approaching midnight. Down below us Saleh gives some final futile jabs, hemmed in as he is by a sea of milling bodies. Two flaring Aladdin lamps illumine the scene, and then the drummer leaps into the small circle and beats out his wild and syncopated rhythm. One by one certain of our workmen are pushed or hauled into the circle. For a moment we can see a rough and poorly clad youth stand awkwardly in the arena, and then he is transfigured, with rhythm flowing through his body and his arms. His actual steps are few, but his whole being is in harmony with the drummer's hands that rap for him a desperate beat to which he quivers in response. There is a quick crescendo and then the drum is muted. He twists and turns a little, but all the time his body is alive with rhythm. Then suddenly, silence; stillness. His dance is over.

Poor Saleh tries to see fair play. There are now perhaps four or five all clamouring to perform. Four are crudely pushed away and a singer stays. 'Alome, Alome, Aloma.' His voice is clearly heard because for a moment the huge crowd is still. They like the strains of Aloma, a merry little love song; and so do we. It is a tune sung so often by the basket boys up on the Tell. Nasal, wavering and strange, the voice subdues us all. Applause. He sings again and then again.

At last they are in their stride; we might be statues on the parapet. The intoxication of the relentless drum, and the singing and the movement, have entered into each one of them. Round dances, solos, songs, follow each other with never an interval between. We, too, become hypnotized; we forget how late it is, how cold it is, how hard the stone. At last the Great Sitt says it all must really stop. We look at our watches and the time is nearly midnight.

'One more, one more, Sitt.'

'No, this is the end.' We all know it is not the end.

'Come again to Jericho and dig for years and years.' This song must be sung. The Great Sitt must reply with a suitable speech in Arabic, and only then can we attempt to struggle to our feet and make our way along the parapet to bed, exhausted but exhilarated.

The Great Sitt's party is of a different genre. We buy half the seats in the local cinema. Our guests mass themselves before the building an hour or so before the show commences, and all eat peanuts and strew the shells everywhere. We arrive about ten minutes before the start, steeling ourselves in readiness for the three hours of unintelligible Arab film that is to follow. One's own particular group of workmen nabs one at the doorway and hustles one into the narrow wooden seats, which are being guarded by other members of the group. There are still a few minutes to go before the lights are dimmed, so our guests avail themselves of the pink drinks and peanuts which by favour of the Great Sitt are now being circulated amongst the audience. We find ourselves with a disgusting drink in one hand, ten peanuts in the other, and then the lights go out. We dare not put the liquid on the floor because already empty glasses are rolling about freely beneath our feet. Peanuts can be dropped one at a time; but this is not of much avail since hot dusky hands are constantly replenishing the unwanted stock in one's own sticky palm. It is best to hold twenty peanuts all through the performance.

The film is about حبيب فاطمه. But we knew before we came that this meant 'Fatima's Lover' and that we were to see for three hours the devotion of a young and wronged maiden, who, in spite of every obstacle, makes her way to her lover's side only to find that he has committed suicide ten minutes before she arrives. The action of the piece, judging from the costume and architecture, could have taken place any time before the present. At the most tense moments – is she or is she not going to be pushed over the parapet? – my neighbour begins labouriously explaining in Arabic, which is as unintelligible as the film dialogue, that Fatima is in great danger. 'Good', I say in the vernacular, meaning 'Yes, I understand', and then I am horrified to see that my simple friend is distressed that I should be so cold-blooded. It is no use trying to explain. Anyway, Fatima is off the balcony now and I try to look as though I knew this was coming and that 'Good' meant 'It will be all right in the end.' And so it goes on – an entertaining nightmare. At eleven p.m. we emerge dazed and bedraggled, only to be accompanied all the way back to the Expedition House by our noisy, happy and grateful guests. I think that, of all we go through at Jericho in the interests of history, perhaps this seasonal film show is the most wearing. One must not for an instant look bored, and that is where the hardship lies.

The days that follow are busy with packing. A few trenches are still being worked upon the Tell, and occasionally we are called out to plan and record a tomb that may have been unearthed by the latrine diggers or the men working on the foundation trenches for the new school. But Dorothy, who is in charge of records and packing, gathers to herself all available hands for the huge task. Enormous wooden crates lie outside the Records Room, a myriad cardboard boxes are piled to the ceiling in nearly every corner – wood shavings, banana leaves, cotton wool, ancient newspapers, clutter all conceivable space.

Old newspapers are a tremendous distraction. Full of good will for the task in hand, I find it difficult to control the eyes, which rove over each sheet as it is whisked from its pile to wrap a jar or be stuffed into the corner of a box. The dignified papers are quite safe. One can pack with them for hours without being led too far astray. We can crumple up leading articles and pictures of politicians without a quiver of curiosity; but the garish 'dreadfuls' are very bad for earnest packers. They lure one on with dizzy photographs and lurid writing. All directors of excavations should be warned of the potential dangers in these papers when they gratefully accept bundles of them 'for packing'.

In fact, getting sufficient material for this task is a serious business. Certain of the crates travel backwards and forwards from England, bringing out fresh stationery and equipment as they return to Jordan each year; but Dorothy has to be charming to her contacts to ensure our supply, and we can all be plunged into despair on her account when she tells us that the very amiable Sergeant

at the Arab Legion station at Amman has been posted,
or that the old proprieter of the banana grove, the
generous provider of dried leaves, is dead. We want so
much, from match boxes to heavy wooden crates, from
tissue paper to wood shavings. All through the dig we
save our cigarettes boxes and it is horrifying to see the
stack. It reminds one of those gastronomic reminders one
sees in encyclopaedias: small man, mountain of potatoes, all
eaten in one year – you know the style of thing. Nevertheless, each year we somehow amass the material, and
all that remains is the task of packing.

The small and delicate objects lie in a tissue paper enve-
lope in a bed of tissue-paper-covered cotton-wool-sausages.
We have been told by packing experts that these sausages
are most important as each one is an individual shock absor-
ber. The normal instinct is to bury a fragile comb in cotton
wool, but this is chancy. The wisps of wool irritate the
surface and there is no division in the mass of padding to
break a shock. A label with the reference goes inside with
the object and another is attached outside each individual
box. The droves of little boxes are packed into bigger
boxes and then into the great crates where jars and bones
lie snugly in their banana leaves and crumpled news-
paper. One huge box is finished. A bold address is painted
on the sides, and we forget about it for the time being
and proceed to fill the next. Most of the crates are
destined for museums in England, but there are others
for countries farther afield: Australia, America, Denmark,
Sweden. Thus our ancient Jerichoans, with certain of
their possessions, leave the Spring by lorry for Jerusalem
to make the long desert journey by train to Akaba,
thence by sea down the Gulf of Akaba to their ultimate
destination. For example, you can see some of our
Middle Bronze Age people now in Birmingham. In the
Museum there one of the tombs has been reconstructed
and the skeletons lie outstretched, as we found them,
with their gifts and pottery vessels just as they were.

Others of our treasures leave by air; but we cannot
always persuade the kindly air magnates that theirs is
by far the best method of transport for very fragile bones

and plastered skulls. They have nevertheless been sympathetic; and Neolithic Jerichoans, packed firmly in cotton wool-sausages, have been flown from Jerusalem to London Airport en route to the anthropologist.

And lastly, certain members of the team carry home the plans, photographs, drawings and notebooks. These are necessary for the work of publication back in England, and we cannot afford the time to let them go on the leisurely voyage by sea.

There was an occasion in the middle of all this packing when Diana and I were called away to salvage a tomb. It was a Roman grave, accidentally found in the cemetery area in the Refugee Village. 'Provincial Roman – oh dear!' That is what is usually said when we have blundered into such burials. We are not digging for Romans, and these intrusive tombs are an interruption. Nevertheless, they too have their story to tell, and this brings me for a moment back to history.

We left Palestine devastated by the armies of Nebuchadnezzar, Jericho a desolate mound, and a vast number of the Hebrews in captivity in Babylon. The people who remained were poor and leaderless, and once again we find the countryside given over to wandering bands and uninspired village builders. For fifty years the tyranny of Babylon retained the exiles; but in 539 B.C. Cyrus, the great Persian, annexed the Empire, and his was a policy of toleration. He allowed the Hebrews to return to Palestine and for the next hundred years groups of them made their way back from Babylon. The temple at Jerusalem was rebuilt, and later, Nehemiah restored the town walls.

But there was friction and uneasiness in the land because the returning Jews despised those who had remained. Racial and religious quarrels broke out among them. Throughout Palestine only a few buildings of the period have survived, and these appear to be official and administrative quarters. The great towns, one by one, ceased to exist and became derelict mounds like Jericho. Megiddo was deserted some time in the fourth century. Samaria lingered on as an administrative centre until it too was forsaken, and the fertile débris of the town was terraced for a garden. The coastal cities fared a little better than the inland town; there is evidence of a varied trade with the Mediterranean lands, particularly with Greece.

In the year 334 B.C. Alexander the Great, then but a youth of twenty-two, overcame the Persians at the battle of Granicus, and at Issus the following year he conquered Darius III, the Great King, refused his peace terms and advanced first through Phoenicia and Palestine into Egypt and later into Persia, and even farther afield to India, building an Empire the like of which had not been known before. With the death of Alexander in 323 B.C. his Empire became disunited and the fate of Palestine, lying between Egypt and Syria, was constantly in dispute. Sometimes the Egyptians and sometimes the Syrians controlled the land. Amidst the factions and squabbles the Jewish Maccabees rallied the Hebrews, and eventually a Jewish Kingdom was established under Hyrcanus, which for sixty-five years, from 129 to 63 B.C., was completely independent. His son Aristobulus (104-103 B.C.) was the first of the line to use the title 'The King of the Jews'. But in the year 63 B.C. there were rival claimants to the throne. Pompey, the Roman general, was petitioned to settle the dispute. Instead of deciding between the two he marched upon Jerusalem, and after a three months' siege, the city fell to him, and he annexed Judaea to the Roman province of Syria. And so the Romans came to Palestine, to the Jordan Valley, to Jericho. The tombs that we have found near the Spring bear witness to this fact.

One particular Roman tomb was located on the edge of the Refugee Village, a hundred yards from the Northern boundary of the Tell. It had been dug into the sloping side of a shallow wadi and consisted of a rectangular forecourt leading through a carefully chiselled doorway in which a great stone door had swung. Beyond, we found the tomb-chamber with three cavernous recesses for the bodies. In these recesses the dead had been placed until it was possible for the bones to be gathered up and stacked into small carved stone boxes. These box urns had no doubt been arranged on the shelves which ran the length of the tomb, but the grave of which I speak had been desecrated. The few boxes that remained were scattered about the floor: some lidless, exposing the neatly packed bones inside; some broken and empty. Throughout the shambles of this tomb were scattered numerous small glass 'tear bottles'. Time and chemical action from the earth had given to each a rainbow lustre. They were exquisite little things, and we wondered that so many of them had survived the trampling feet and greedy hands of the tomb robbers. The roof of the tomb had been weathered away: so, once more, we were working in an open pit round which an admiring audience squatted for hours on end.

Since we were right on the edge of the Village, by a road which skirted the Tell to the gipsy encampment at the back, we were often visited by the wild nomadic tinkers. The women wear black and boldly stare one in the eye. There is no veil-pulling reticence about them. They stride up to our hole and salute us with great bonhomie. If one or other of us is unlucky enough to be outside the tomb at the time of visitation, the chances are we will have our arms patted and clothes plucked to the accompaniment of a great deal of chatter, either of approval or disapproval (we have never been able to fathom which).

But we in our turn discuss them, mainly their nose rings, which fascinate us. One ring was at least two inches in diameter and was weighted down by a roughly cut turquoise. Our blowsy friend knew quite well we were admiring her jewel, and she whipped it out to show us the tiny hook at one end which passed through her nose to catch a small loop on the other end. The fastening is always inside the nostril. I was relieved to see that it came in and out so easily: I had imagined these poor women with permanent rings in their noses.

Our standards of comfort are so different from theirs, however, that it is impossible to know how and when to sympathize. Certain of the little girls in the Refugee

Village have not got their own traditional veils: they wear, quite happily and inappropriately, the pink bath towels issued to them by the charitable organization in charge of clothing and stores. They appear oblivious to comfort.

Our Roman tomb was not unique; we have had others. But nothing now remains of the town of Roman times. Certainly it was not built upon the Tell, which must have been a barren landmark by the Spring.

Josephus, the Jewish historian, gives us vivid accounts of Herod's skirmishes in the Valley near Jericho and of his rise to power, backed up by Rome. As King, he built a palace here, but not near our ancient town. He chose to build his Winter Residence a mile away, to the south of the deserted mound. But the water of the Spring still fed the fields about the Tell and made a rich oasis in this wilderness. We are told that the 'palm trees, both many in number and excellent in kind' attracted the greedy eyes of Cleopatra, as also did the balsam, which was much sought after as a drug and could be obtained from balsam-producing trees here at Jericho. Josephus tells us how her poor bedevilled Anthony was persuaded 'to take those dominions away from their several princes and bestow them upon her: and she had a mighty influence upon him by reason of his being enslaved to her by his affections.... As for Anthony, he was so entirely overcome by this woman that one would not think her conversation alone could do it but that he was some way or other bewitched to do whatsoever she would have him.... She accompanied Anthony in his expedition to Armenia, as far as Euphrates; she returned back and came to Apamia and Damascus, and passed on to Judea where Herod met her and farmed to her parts of Arabia and those revenues that came to her from the region about Jericho.'[1]

Josephus tells us that she stayed with Herod at his Palace. Her chariot may have passed along the foot of the mound as she drove abroad to survey her possessions in the oasis. It was all hers, given to her by Anthony.

[1] *The Genuine Works of Flavius Josephus.* By the late Wm. Whiston, M.A. J. Grigg, Philadelphia, 1829.

Little did she know that the desert slope concealed the
treasures of Middle Bronze Age tombs; her eyes would
only have assessed the wealth to be gained from the
luxuriant growth of the balsam and the palms.

How Herod hated her! While she was with him at
Jericho he contemplated murder; but he was afraid of
Anthony – of Rome.

And then in time the Romans, too, retreated from the
Valley. Our great mound sprawled there by the Spring:
a secret, dead and forgotten city. Jericho – it was the first
of all towns; it had known greatness; and it had known
defeat. Within its bounds thousands of human beings
had lived and toiled and died. It brooded through the
centuries, a dead thing, and kept its secrets until our days.

Much happened in the Valley in all those years since
the Roman times, but no one bothered with the sleeping
town, until an Englishman called Warren, in the middle
of the last century, thought he would investigate. He
dug several deep well-like pits right down into the mound
and reported that he could find nothing of much interest.
Here his labours ended.

Then, in 1907, began the first of the three big expeditions that between them have begun to wrest Jericho's
secrets from the earth and are giving to the world its
story. The first expedition was sponsored by the Germans
and was led by Watzinger; the second, a British expedition in the 'thirties, was directed by Professor John Garstang; and the third and present expedition is led, as I
have said, by Dr Kathleen Kenyon.

For four years now Dr Kenyon's team has burrowed
into the mound, peeling away the centuries, as we peel
away the layers of human occupation that lie one upon
the other. Deeper and deeper we go and farther and
farther back in time we take the story. Although we
have dug down to the natural rock and found the first
wall, we are outside that wall; what lies inside has still
to be uncovered.

And so, in our turn at the end of each season, with our
treasures packed away, we prepare to leave the Valley.
In groups or singly the members of the team set out upon

their travels home. Some wish to journey slowly, visiting the great sites in Syria and in Greece. Others plan a route through Turkey and beyond.

By degrees the tents come down, and everywhere there are bundles to be stored. Much of our stuff is most generously stowed away by the American School of Oriental Research in Jerusalem; but much remains at Jericho itself. At the very end, the doorways and certain of the windows are walled up with mud bricks and the Camp House is sealed.

As we leave the Spring and the ancient town, many of our workmen gather about the cars to say goodbye. Those of them who work upon the Tell walk back along the water channels to modern stone-built Jericho; but our tomb-diggers are refugees. They have no stone houses of a modern kind; theirs is the huge mud town of the Encampment, where they are already accumulating the first layer of a new Tell. The mud of their houses is already dissolving — always mud bricks are being made and carried into the Village; their water pots are breaking and being forgotten; little dolls and treasures, that will one day be 'mother goddesses' and 'amulets', are slipping into the mud. New floors, new hearths, new walls — the pattern is just the same. And although more than seven thousand years separate them from their precursors of Layer I at the bottom of the Tell, their way of living cannot have altered very much. What is a Primus stove more or less?